LIZ S

3G

MENTORING

A RELATIONAL STRATEGY
FOR WORKING WITH

GENERATIONAL
DISTINCTIONS

GLOBAL
DIVERSITY

GENDER
DIFFERENCES

Published by Mentor Leadership Team

www.mentorleadershipteam.com

Editorial Direction by Caleb Seeling, Samizdat Creative Services, Denver, CO

www.samizdatcreative.com

Cover and Interior Design by Amber D. Strickler, Curiously Wired Consulting, Denver, CO

www.curiouslywiredds.com

ISBN 978-0-578-08429-9

Printed in Canada.

3G

MENTORING

MENTOR LEADERSHIP TEAM

CONTENTS

THE THREE G'S

"Mentoring is such a waste of time!" I inwardly groaned when I heard that I had to find a mentor in order to finish my master's degree. My time was already packed with other responsibilities—family, work, and school—so adding a time-consuming mentoring relationship seemed like an unnecessary addition. But within a few years, I went from being dragged kicking and screaming into a mentoring relationship to completing my dissertation about the importance of mentoring! I found that mentoring is a powerful tool for leadership development, training, and encouragement in organizations. This is especially true when jobs are tight and people are being asked to take on more tasks and step into more roles than ever.

I have become passionate about teaching and training people how to mentor, and the organizations I have worked with have seen dramatic improvements in their workforce, including increased employee engagement, reduced turnover, better organizational communication, increased motivation, and growth in the appreciation of peoples' strengths, which lead to higher organizational performance.

Recently, some colleagues and I started The Mentor Leadership Team (MLT) (www.mentorleadershipteam.com), which focuses on specific challenges of the organizational landscape that seem to be causing conflict and reduced productivity in businesses and organizations. As competition for jobs has become more acute, certain challenges have become more pronounced. We call them the **three G's**:

• **Generational Distinctions**—With four generations currently in the workplace, inevitable clashes of values and ways of doing business have increased.

• **Global Diversity**—As electronic media and globalization has flattened the world, this new landscape means: you must be even more nimble to keep up with the constant change, which makes stable adjustments difficult.[1] Cultural differences are readily apparent, potentially affecting business efficacy.

• **Gender Differences**—While men and woman experience more equity in the workplace than they have in the past, understanding what traits each gender brings to the table, and how to use the strengths of each, can increase an organization's stability and effectiveness.

Mentoring is a critical strategy to leverage the three G's into synergies rather than conflicts, promoting a dynamic, engaged workforce rather than a disconnected, unmotivated one. We have seen that a mentoring culture, where people are valued and life-long learning is the norm, ultimately adds to an organization's bottom line.

We believe mentoring will take:

ORGANIZATIONS:
From Conflicting, Ineffective ⟶ To Synergistic, Productive

AND EMPLOYEES:
From Disconnected, Unmotivated ⟶ To Dynamic, Engaged

MLT values mentoring, leadership development, and synergistic teamwork. As a result, we see the critical need for *3G Mentoring: an Integrated Approach to Building Dynamic Organizational Cultures.*

Research shows that 78% of learning is informal and that social learning enhances employee productivity, flexibility, creativity, and the speed and quality of business.[2] It has also been proven that heterogeneous groups perform better than homogeneous ones do, and an engaged mentoring culture is a sure strategy to promote diversity and help employees appreciate and learn to use the differences among them.

So it's easy to see that a comprehensive and encouraging mentoring culture is critical to keep your organization diverse and innovative. With the synergies harnessed by 3G mentoring, your organization can become more nimble and remain competitive in today's constantly changing market.

PART ONE

THE BASICS

SECTION 1

THE BASICS OF MENTORING

WHAT YOU PROBABLY NEED TO KNOW

Mentoring has been around as long as human relationships have thrived. The term "mentor" comes from the ancient classic *The Odyssey,* in which Odysseus's son Telemachus was cared for and guided by a companion named Mentor. Later, under the medieval guild system, craftsmen passed down their livelihood to their children or others through apprenticeship. Today, mentoring is used in youth work, education, health care, religious groups, and just about any type of business setting. Mentoring is gaining notoriety as a solid business practice and is a "buzz" word in many for-profit and non-profit businesses.

Mentoring does not need to be a complicated process or program. In fact, within certain parameters and given good preparation, it is one of the most basic, organic forms of training available. Because so many people today are isolated, apathetic, alienated, and scared, mentoring can be a great way to connect, encourage, and motivate your workforce through proactive relationships.

> *"If you want to go fast, go alone; if you want to go far, go together." —African proverb*

According to Mark Paskowitz, a senior consultant with The Ken Blanchard Companies, the best leaders are those who encourage.

Other traits come in to play, but this is a constant. "There is a difference between showing up at work and people doing their best work," he says.[3] Trust in leadership erodes and performance suffers when the efforts of your people aren't recognized. Mentoring helps move organizations away from rigid power structures by focusing on developing individual potential through encouragement and relational support.

Consequently, through encouragement, employees are more likely to do their best work. They are more engaged, they see that their efforts matter, and they are happy to be moving forward professionally. When people can see that you authentically care about helping them do their best, they feel safer and valued. They will allow their passion for their work to surface in powerful ways, opening up opportunities for creative solutions and innovation, which is critical in today's rapidly changing market.

Mentoring is critical to leadership development and it can work in any context where people work together. It can be done across distance, with all generations, genders and global cultures, and with all skill levels. Mentoring literally creates an exponential knowledge expansion and limitless skill development opportunities.

What about when the economy turns south?

Mentoring provides a much stronger model for learning and growth than a one-time seminar or conference. During an economic downturn, mentoring can keep motivation high and engagement strong, maximizing current talent. A mentor can supply ongoing help and encouragement to apply concepts to everyday work life.

Team mentoring seems to work particularly well in business recovery scenarios.[4] Alison Carter of the Institute of Employment Studies notes that coaching and mentoring have held up in the recession, even as other discretionary development activities have been cut.[5] Coaching and mentoring were found by the British Broadcasting Company to compare favorably to other types of training and investments into human resource and leadership development.[6] Lily Benavides found that 87% of training dollars are wasted after thirty days if follow-up coaching or mentoring is not provided.[7] From the most basic financial arguments, mentoring is a strong human resource development strategy.

> *NASA found that what makes good systems engineers great is the softer people skills that can be developed through mentoring.*

Let's get going, then

Now, this all sounds great, but it is important to understand certain things about how to launch mentoring in your organization. All levels of management need to be involved in the overall mentoring strategy. This way everyone will move together in the same general direction, even if each individual path looks slightly different. This will also keep line managers, for instance, from picking very different goals than executive managers, causing inevitable and unnecessary conflict. Individuals should have guidance in selecting mentoring goals that fit them personally, as well as the organization's strategic goals.

THE BENEFITS OF MENTORING

In a successful mentoring program, it is important for everyone involved to buy in whole-heartedly. To do this, all parties should understand and believe in the benefits of participating. Many of these benefits are listed below.

• **For the mentor:** Reinforces accomplishments, expands sphere of influence, enhances communication skills and learning, provides a way to reciprocate or give back, promotes leaving a legacy, increases recognition, allows for investment, increases the personal satisfaction of making a difference.

• **For the mentee:** Expands sphere of influence, enhances communication and decision-making skills, improves time management and career development, reduces burnout by helping people find an integrated work and life balance, helps work through ambiguity and constantly changing environments, increases confidence and faster learning of organizational culture, skills, and attitudes, promotes visibility, and increases the feeling of being valued.

• **For the organization:** Gives a recruiting edge through exposure to organizations and a sense of community, increases participation and engagement of employees, manages stress and change while promoting higher productivity, aligns the organization's goals with personal goals of the employees (which may also help garner support for new organizational initiatives and transitions), improves motivation, raises productivity through specific goal setting, reduces turnover and enhances satisfaction (people leave people, not jobs), enhances communication, reduces organizational silos, provides a faster and more robust transfer of knowledge and skills, increases loyalty and retention, provides for better succession planning, promotes organizational brand

MENTORING INTEGRATION

Theresa* was troubled by a lack of assertiveness in her personal life. Her mentor began to see how this also overflowed into her work relationships, preventing her innovative ideas from being heard. Working with Theresa to be more assertive in volunteer activities and family relationships was a safe practice ground for assertiveness training without harming her career. This was particularly important since the company was going through financial challenges. As Theresa became more comfortable voicing her innovative ideas in safe situations, she gradually began to voice them at work, where they were subsequently heard and used. The end result was noteworthy support to the organization in terms of new innovation. One idea in particular changed the company's pricing structure in a way that brought in new business. This mentoring relationship helped Theresa integrate her life, practice skills in a safe environment, move her forward professionally, and substantially benefit her organization.

*Names and identifying details for "In Action" scenarios have been changed to protect confidentiality.

identity, offers inclusion through more positive relationships within a diverse organizational culture.

FAILURE TO MENTOR

The organization I worked for had a corporate culture of long work hours and emphasis on work relationships. When Grace was hired onto the senior leadership team, thanks to her striking résumé, we were all excited about the potential her addition would add. Unfortunately, she was never mentored into our particular corporate culture. Long hours and open doors were a must for senior leadership, but Grace would work with her door closed and no one really knew when she was there or not. It also made her seem unfriendly and unapproachable. This subtle disrespect for the organizational culture and lack of connection eventually was her undoing as even her team did not support her, her ideas, or her efforts. She left the organization frustrated, her skills never really appreciated or utilized.

Individuals and organizations benefit in very specific ways through mentoring. Research supports the advantages of utilizing a mentoring strategy. A few recent findings are on the following page:

MENTORING STATISTICS

• The Emerging Workforces study cites that 77% of companies that support mentoring saw an increase in retention and an increase in performance.[8]

• The Saratoga Institute reports that 50% of job satisfaction is related to an employee's relationship with her immediate supervisor.[9] Mentoring and coaching strengthen this.

• Workforce Management cites that 96% of surveyed businesses reported mentoring as an important developmental tool.[10]

• In a study done by Manchester Incorporated, the ROI is typically six times the cost when coaching and mentoring is provided to those in management—well worth the effort. A recent study showed that 78% of organizations do not evaluate the ROI on leadership development programs.[11]

• Gallup research found that 29% of staff in secular organizations were "engaged," which means that 71% are "disengaged clock watchers," and 21% of employees were "highly disengaged" at the end of 2009, up from 8% in the first half of 2007.[12] Mentoring is a powerful tactic to increase engagement and stop the clockwatching!

• The Harvard Business Review reported that 70% of today's high performers lack critical attributes essential to their success in future roles. Nearly 40% of internal job moves involving high potential employees end in failure.[13] You must be proactive in engaging high performers in relationships that encourage, challenge, educate, and train, ultimately helping them to see their vital part in the organization, giving them a sense of purpose, and encouraging their desire to stay.

• Alison Carter from the Institute for Employment Studies reports: "The BBC estimated that the cost of the coaching through its in-house network was only £50 per hour, which compare very favorably to other training investments in a company's human capital."[14]

• In a study I did on graduate students, 81% of them found their mentoring relationship helpful/very helpful in their graduate work, and a significant correlation was found between these students and those who continued in mentoring relationships after their graduate studies were completed.[15]

WHAT EXACTLY IS MENTORING?

I think Lois Zachary, author of *Creating a Mentoring Culture*, defines it best:

> *A reciprocal and collaborative learning relationship between two (or more) individuals who share mutual responsibility and accountability for helping a mentee work toward achievement of clear and mutually-defined learning goals.[16]*

Coaching vs. mentoring

At this point it may sound like mentoring is a lot like coaching, and there are many similarities. Both coaching and mentoring are about hiring the right people, developing the right people, and inspiring the right people. Neither coaching nor mentoring are about creating a "mini-you." Both can be a trainer and learning coordinator/promoter. Both mentors and coaches can mobilize, connect, and support. Both coaches and mentors focus on expanding the potential of an individual, helping him or her to expand influence, and ultimately contribute to the growth of the organization.

But coaching and mentoring are different in important ways. Mentoring tends to be more organic, and evolves over time. There is often more mutuality in mentoring than in coaching. Mentoring is more of a pull than a push, while coaching is more prescribed and focuses most on performance and skill evaluation than on personal transformation. Coaches are often outside hires because they have the objectivity needed to focus on skill building. Mentors are often found within the organization so that modeling and sponsorship can be maximized.

> *"Part of our purpose in life is to build legacy—a consistent pattern of building into the lives of others." —Tony Dungy*

Informal versus formal programs

Mentoring can be effective whether or not a formal program is implemented by an organization. Informal mentoring naturally happens when people look to others as role models, when they ask for encouragement or help in developing a skill, when differing perspectives are seen as ways to thoroughly examine options and learn from them, and when a more seasoned employee helps a new hire understand corporate culture.

ADDED BENEFITS

I've seen over and over that, where formal mentoring programs have been instituted, employees and managers report a general awareness of mentoring that encourages more informal mentoring to take place. This mentoring culture then improves communication across departments, increases constructive learning, and heightens the sense of community.

Business expert John Darling asserts that the five core informal learning processes (which I see employed regularly in an informal mentoring culture) are:

• Watching and listening: Observing what works and what doesn't, how to behave, who's who, and so on.

• Conversing: Learning from talking with peers (what is appropriate and expected).

• Trial and error: Learning by doing.

• Being coached: Being guided by someone with some type of authority (like a boss, parent, subject matter expert (SME), and others).

• Seeking: An individual taking the initiative to learn something new (sometimes through internal motivation, sometimes through external motivation).[17]

> *"Seldom ever was any knowledge given to keep, but to impart; the grace of this rich jewel is lost in concealment." —Wendel Phillips*

On the other hand, formal mentoring can take a number of forms, but the basic idea is that organizational leaders create structured mentoring relationships. They may help with pairing mentees and mentors, or perhaps invest in an official launch of the program beginning with basic training in mentoring skills. The program coordinator evaluates the program's effectiveness when the program as a whole is over and makes recommendations for future efforts. Formal mentoring programs succeed when the ongoing mentoring relationships are given the proper resources and support. We'll talk more about how to create a formal program later in this section.

Web mentoring

Web mentoring is where people in mentoring relationships (whether formal or informal) interact with and draw from other mentees and mentors. A participant is often a mentor and a mentee at the same time. Participants can help others develop new skills while at the same time enhancing their own skill set. This creates a vibrant web of relationships and learning.

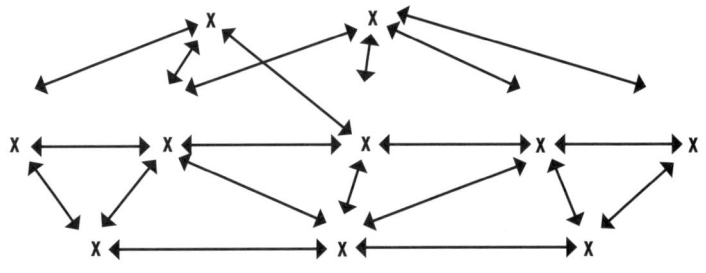

> *"Leaders develop daily, not in a day."*
> *—John C. Maxwell*

The goal—a mentoring culture

When informal and formal mentoring are a way of life for an organization, it supports a mentoring culture. This, in my opinion, should be the goal of every organization—to get to the point when employees can't remember a time when active mentoring was not a vital part of doing business. Nothing is lost with more information, more learning, acceptance of diverse perspectives, clearer communication…you get the picture!

WHAT MAKES AN EFFECTIVE MENTORING RELATIONSHIP?

If you know what an effective mentor or mentee looks like, it gives you a standard to aspire to. My personal research and experience, and that of the mentoring industry, has shown the following:

Characteristics of an effective mentor: An effective mentor is a good listener, authentic, trustworthy, wise (has something to offer), understands the power of a good question over a good piece of information, is skilled in giving feedback, committed, insightful, inspiring, has a tolerance for mistakes, shows flexibility and patience, is discerning, is able to set boundaries, has a learning attitude, and has learned from his or her own successes and failures.

> *"Nothing is so infectious as an example."*
> *—Charles Kingsley*

Characteristics of an effective mentee: An effective mentee is ready and motivated to grow and learn, is open and honest, dependable, takes initiative, is available, trustworthy, passionate, a good listener, follows through, is committed, shows consistency, and is open to other's perspectives.

IN ACTION

NO "MINI-ME"

Mentoring is not about creating a "mini-me." I found this out the hard way. In one of my first attempts to mentor someone, I assumed that my mentee's success should look like mine and that the steps I took would automatically work for her. We wasted so much time and she became frustrated, doubting her abilities since success didn't seem to come to her as it had for me. I realized that we are all too different to apply the specifics of success for one person directly to another. Sharing successes is fine, but mentors should be careful not to think that mentees should follow exactly in their footsteps. Mentees are too different and need to find their unique path to success that utilizes their unique strengths and experiences. Mentors are to be an example of strength and determination, supporting mentees in the discovery of their own path to success, and encouraging them along that path to reach their highest potential.

It is important for the mentee to be the driver of the mentoring relationship. Mentees who are confident and take responsibility for the learning outcomes of the mentoring relationship can be relaxed, open, and curious, able to see their strengths and weaknesses without being defensive. They can handle mistakes with grace and a realistic long-term perspective. Mentees need to tailor their mentoring activities so that they make sense, are achievable, and so that they are motivated to complete. The mentor's suggestions and guidance are important, but if the mentee does not desire to change and grow, then change will not occur.

Characteristics of an effective mentoring relationship: An effective mentoring relationship is reciprocal, trustworthy and confidential, accountable, and includes time spent together in varied contexts. It includes listening, respect, clear expectations, and is evaluated regularly so that improvements or challenges are noted and worked on.

A strong mentoring relationship promotes understanding the organizational culture, expands networks, increases confidence in skills, promotes lifestyle integration, leadership development, business and technical skills, relationship skills, and communication effectiveness.

As you look at the above lists, are there some qualities you know you possess? Write them here:

_____
_____
_____

Are there some that you know you will probably need to work on? Write them here:

_____
_____
_____

Mentoring **is not** a standardized, one-size-fits-all process.
Mentoring **is** an individualized personal investment.

Mentoring **is not** a plan for the mentee to become just like the mentor.
Mentoring **is** encouraging mentees to become all they can be.

Mentoring **is not** the mentor's agenda.
Mentoring **is** developing and supporting the mentee's agenda.

Mentoring **is not** giving all the mentor's knowledge, opinions, and advice to a clueless mentee.
Mentoring **is** coming alongside another person to help them find their own strengths, grow in their ability to make informed decisions, and perform to the best of their ability.

> *"If I could offer one piece of advice to all students, it would be to seek a mentor. If I could offer a second: become a mentor."*
> *—Prof. Steven Lerman, Vice Chancellor for Graduate Studies, MIT*

SETTING UP A FORMAL PROGRAM

Mentoring is a powerful tool for change, but if it's done poorly it can cause more harm than good. More accountability and access to organizational resources is built into formal mentoring programs. They can spur growth in employees and allow the organization to influence the learning that takes place. This is helpful because the organization can then align personal goals with organizational ones. Thinking through a mentoring program's goals and preparing well can ensure a successful transition to a mentoring culture.

> *"Happiness is not so much in having as in sharing. We make a living by what we get, but we make a life by what we give."*
> *—Norman McEwan*

The following will give an overview of the steps involved in setting up a mentoring program and the skills needed by both mentors and mentees to promote healthy and productive mentoring relationships.

The steps to create a formal mentoring program are:

1. Establishing processes and expectations

Setting up realistic and specific expectations for the mentoring program in general and the mentoring relationships in particular is critical for a successful program (e.g., when you will meet, what type of goals you will accomplish, how you will give each other feedback). See "Exercises" at the end of this section for templates to set up expectations.

Matching mentees and mentors is also important. There are a number of ways to accomplish this:

• You may let pairs find each other. A version of "speed dating" with prospective mentors and mentees has been used with success.

• You select the pairs yourself (e.g., pairing new hires with more seasoned employees).

• You may want to eliminate silos in your organization by promoting communication and understanding between certain areas. This should fit with the strategic purpose of the formal mentoring program and can be orchestrated from the mentoring program coordinators' end.

• A number of companies sell software that can help you match people based on certain criteria or by compatibility (e.g., MentorSphere™, Optimatch™).

2. Building the relationship

In the first few meetings between the mentee and mentor, the primary task is to build trust. The five skills of a mentee and mentor (explained in more detail below) are used in earnest.

3. Developing the mentee

This stage is where the pairs will spend the bulk of their time. The five skills will continue to be used, but this is where development, growth, and change really take place. It's where planned learning activities are put into practice and where encouragement and corrective feedback move the mentee forward.

> *"Before you are a leader, success is all about growing yourself. When you become a leader, success is all about growing others."*
> —Jack Welch

4. Evaluation/ celebration/ recommendation

Formal mentoring relationships need an end point. While some pairings may continue informally for an additional span of time, designating an ending point to the formal relationship gives mentees and mentors the chance to evaluate what happened, celebrate successes, and look at recommendations for the mentee's progress in the future.

Mentoring should be evaluated for how effective the process was for individual development and progress toward business goals. Discuss what went well, what business best practices should be implemented, what challenges were experienced and how they were overcome, and what changes should be made for the future. Act on the appropriate recommendations so that people are encouraged to continue providing feedback.

Be sure to ask for positive stories you can use to build the program's momentum. Summarize the results of the program for organizational learning. Celebrate the successes to solidify the positives of the experience and make the participants feel like their time was well spent. Formal celebration creates a positive buzz about what was accomplished and enjoyed during the mentoring program so that it continues to gain traction within your organization.

 IN ACTION

CRITICAL CELEBRATION

A number of organizations I work with have done a great job celebrating their mentoring programs. Not only do they have a great "end of program" party, but some of them caught successful mentoring stories on video to inspire other people in the organization about how powerful and career-changing the experience had been. These videos helped the programs gain not only positive status, but momentum for future mentoring efforts.

BASIC MENTORING SKILLS

Becoming an effective mentor and a proficient mentee is something that can be taught. Eric Thompson, of the Thompson Leadership Group, asserts, "'I don't have time to mentor' is usually a cover for 'I don't know how.' The leader who allows this mentality to prevail is choosing comfort over progress."[18] By training people in the five basic skills of mentoring, your organization will reap the rewards of personal and organizational development.

I have found that these five basic skills, if practiced by both mentors and mentees, help the mentoring relationship run much more smoothly. I have adapted these from a more extensive model created by Dr. Linda Phillips-Jones of The Mentoring Group.[19] Her model looks at both mentee/mentor shared skills and mentee/mentor specific skills. Her model is extremely helpful. I have found in training, however, that by keeping the skills to five shared skills, the focus then becomes the reciprocal nature of the relationship. It opens the door much more widely for mentees not only to learn from their mentors, but also for the mentors to learn from their mentees. At the most basic level, these skills are about respect and appreciation for your mentoring partner.

SKILL NO. 1
LISTENING EFFECTIVELY

The first skill is listening effectively. Listening, truly giving others our full attention, is one of the greatest things you can do for

LISTENING EFFECTIVELY

I remember one of the first mentors I had (although the mentor tag was not used) was a man who listened to me as teenager. I had felt so invisible and unimportant, but he listened to me and remembered my name at a time when I felt invisible. It was a relationship that literally changed the trajectory of my life from self-destruction to believing I mattered. Today, this type of attention is just as valuable, if not more. Americans are not particularly great listeners (Unfortunately, I have to include myself in this statistic), but listening to others is critical to fruitful relationships. Listening affirms others, encourages them, and builds the trust necessary for growth.

them. It validates your feelings and passions and helps you understand more fully your desired goals.

To listen effectively, begin by checking your internal motivations, conflicts, biases, and so on. Acknowledge these issues and try to not bring them into your mentoring conversations. In this way, you will be able to listen with as little of a filter as possible. Impatience caused by negative biases or misunderstandings can be read easily and will hurt the establishment of trust, which is necessary for growth.

Pay attention to how other people listen to you. As you talk, notice what bothers you about how the other person is listening. Then try avoid those behaviors yourself when it's your turn to listen. In addition, take note of what you appreciate as you are listened to. Then practice those behaviors as other people talk to you. This isn't rocket science, but it does take intentionality. I have found it helpful to do two things:

• Quiet inside: Recognize inner dialogues, biases, daily frustrations. Try to put them on the shelf while you are with your mentoring partner.

• Quiet outside: Find a place without distractions and that is neutral. Watch your non-verbal cues so they encourage openness rather than disinterest.

> *"Fame is based on what we get in life, but true greatness is based on what we give in life."*
> *—Mark Sanborne, The Fred Factor*

SKILL NO. 2
BUILDING TRUST

The second skill is building trust, which is probably the most critical element of organizational, team, and leadership effectiveness. Trust is formed by our experiences and is based on our perception of someone else's behaviors. Sadly, only 39% of US employees trust their senior leaders, and only 20% of US employees trust the organization they work for.[20] There is clearly a trust deficit in organizations today. Turnover is often based on whether an employee trusts his or her immediate supervisor. People without trust may actually "quit" emotionally and yet physically stay on the job. This is a worst-case scenario for productivity; lack of trust eventually translates into lack of customers.

Trust is the basis on which growth and learning occur. Without it, mentoring relationships are crippled and will most likely be ineffective. One way to build trust is to align our actions with our beliefs and values. Steven Covey uses the analogy of an emotional bank account: You cannot withdraw more than you deposit. You must establish a strong relationship first, and that will support the challenges that may surface later.[21]

The most effective managers are able to suspend their biases and put themselves in the shoes of the people they manage. Espinoza, Ukleja, and Rusch's 2010 study asserts that the most effective managers talked about their own need to change in order to manage well in today's world. They believed there was something they could do about the challenges at work and they allowed their subordinates to challenge them (ideas, structures, and pro-

 **IN ACTION**

TRUST BUSTED

Greg was walking into the office when Darrin, one of his mentee's friends, approached and told him how much he admired him. Greg was confused since he had never directly talked with Darrin. Darrin said that he had come from an alcoholic family and was impressed that Greg had opted to not drink since he had also come from an acoholic family.

Greg knew that alcohol problems were considered a weakness in his organization, and he had never wanted this part of his past to be discussed. He had told his mentee, Brian, in confidence about his past as an illustration of how to overcome an earlier issue. Now he was worried that if this story got out, he would be sidelined in an upcoming promotion. He was also very upset with Brian for sharing such potentially volatile information.

Greg went to Brian to ask why he had shared this confidential story. Brian was horrified when he realized that what he had shared with Darrin had disrespected Greg and upset him so much. He told Greg he had only told the story to encourage Darrin because he was so impressed with how Greg had handled things. Greg affirmed Brian's positive motivation, but told Brian that it would be a while before that trust could be rebuilt. They both reaffirmed their commitment to confidentiality, and Brian followed up quickly with Darrin so that the story did not spread.

cesses); using the power of relationship versus the power of their position to encourage those they work with.[22]

Here are some of the best ways to build trust:
• Uphold confidentiality.
• Always follow through.
• Show open regard for people and regard for what they are trying to accomplish.
• Stay open and authentic.
• Believe in your mentoring partner and that they have the best intentions.

Also, observe things that seem to be a trigger, either positive or negative. Discuss them with your mentee or mentor. Don't be afraid to really challenge them—working through difficult circumstances and tough challenges bonds people together.

This brings up the important topic of effective conflict management. Dealing with conflict in a healthy manner is critical to building trust. You can't have growth without differing perspectives and, in some cases, actual conflict. And you can't have different perspectives honestly represented without disagreement or conflict. So here are a few tips for how to use conflict to strengthen your mentoring relationship:

• Say it early—don't let bad feelings fester.

• Use the "I", not "you." Make it about how you are reacting rather than about what you think the other person thinks. More often than not you will be wrong about what exactly he/she is thinking—you are not your mentoring partner. By the same token, no one can argue with how you perceived things. What you saw is what you saw. The discussion then is based on individual perceptions rather than on "right" or "wrong."

• Affirm first, and then talk about misperceptions and differing opinions.

• Dealing with conflict gets easier over time and within a culture that supports it.

• Own (be aware of) your tension so you don't display it overtly. High emotion feeds on itself. Take the tension down so that cooler heads will prevail.

• Be specific with the issues of the conflict so that specific solutions can be found.

• Come up with a plan together.

> *"If there are not regular disagreements, I know, as a leader, I've not engaged people fully." —John Ortberg*

One last issue with building trust between mentors and mentees—mentees should avoid trying to "snow" their mentors, especially if they have picked the mentor for political reasons. This relationship is doomed from the start because true growth occurs in a safe and honest environment where trust has been established.

SKILL NO. 3
DEVELOPING GROWTH PLANS AND STRATEGIC GOAL SETTING

The third skill is strategic goal setting and well thought-out growth plans, which are critical to a formal mentoring program. They allow the program to be evaluated on concrete terms related to growth and progress. If goals are not set, it is difficult to ascertain whether the program was beneficial for the individuals and the organization beyond the positive evaluation of a relationship that went well. Don't worry, growth plans and goal setting aren't as difficult or intimidating as they sound. Here are a few easy tips:

• Just do it: Don't just read or talk about what you want to do—put compelling goals and plans in place so that action can take place.

• Tailor it to the specific mentee: Use learning techniques and methods that best suit your mentees' learning styles, skills, talents, strengths, and organizational roles.

• Build in accountability: Mentors should do their best to avoid judgment, control, and ownership of the mentees' issues. What mentors can provide is the accountability of being there regularly to discuss both progress and challenges. Mentors cannot do for mentees what mentees must do for themselves. Help mentees recover from commitment failures and move forward through encouragement by reminding them that you believe in them.

What makes people successful is self-discipline over time, supported by accountability.

• Focus on strengths: Buckingham and Clifton highlight the importance of working in your area of strength more than in your weaknesses, pointing out that people grow most in their areas of strength.[23] So, when possible, mentors can help mentees work in their areas of strength and surround themselves with people who are strong in their areas of weakness.

Globally, only 20% of workers feel they use their strengths every day.[24] This means that 80% are not tapping into their full poten-

SUCCESSION BASED ON STRENGTHS

The old idea of succession was about replacing yourself with someone just like you—a one-to-one type of replacement. I have found that this rarely works, since no two people are alike or possess identical skill sets. In many organizations (including some I have been a part of) when people leave due to voluntary choice, downsizing, or firing, often what happens is that the roles and tasks left behind are forced upon those who remain. What I found much more successful when dealing with succession and filling in the gaps is developing a pool of leaders who will step in as their skills, talents, and experiences are needed. Even though job responsibilities may need to be rearranged to address the new constellation of skill sets, people are much more productive in the end when they are working in their areas of strength.

tial. Appreciation of strengths can be synergistic as everyone, acting in their "sweet spot," produces passion and increases productivity.

Setting SMART Goals

Taking strategic goal setting a step further, utilizing SMART goal criteria has become an industry standard. Research shows that creating goals based on these criteria are met more often than those goals that aren't SMART. Use the acrostic S-M-A-R-T to evaluate whether your goals are written in a compelling manner:

• **Specific:** A goal needs to be specific in order to develop concrete steps that will lead to it. Just saying, *"I want to be a better athlete"* doesn't tell anyone how to actually become a better athlete. Rather than saying, *"I will train so that I can run a half-marathon,"* lay out some specifics like, *"I will run 10 miles 5 days per week for the first month."* The specific goal must also be applicable —*"I will put together a timeline of runs leading up to a scheduled half-marathon"* is more appropriate than *"throwing a shot putt four times a week"* for actually getting ready to run a half-marathon.

• **Measurable:** A goal needs to be measurable or you will never be able to assess if you are achieving it. Progress toward the goal *"I will become a better speaker"* can be tracked easily if you say, *"I want to become a speaker whose evaluations from attendees are rated good or very good for 80% of the respondents. And I will use an outline rather than reading word-for-word from a script."* It will be easy to determine whether or not these goals were met.

• **Achievable:** A goal needs to be challenging, but not defeating. It needs to stretch the mentees, but not be so far out of their reach that they don't even try to achieve it. Sometimes a goal can be more achievable if they are given more time to accomplish it, or if it is broken down into smaller pieces. *"I'll earn my PhD next week"* is clearly unachievable, but *"I will earn my PhD in five years,"* or *"I will apply for a PhD program next week"* may be achievable.

• **Relevant:** A goal must be applicable and meaningful to the mentee. If mentees are dragging their feet, it often may be because the goal is not relevant to them. Listening carefully to your mentees and helping them craft a meaningful goal they are motivated to complete will generate better results and more satisfaction. Unfortunately, some mentors help craft goals that would work for themselves rather than for the mentee. Since the mentee is a different person with different experiences and skills, that transfer does not always work. Mentees should take the lead in the specific aspects of the goal so that the goal is meaningful to them.

• **Time-bound:** A goal needs a clear endpoint or it may never be accomplished. Without a deadline, a goal is easier to delay. Keep in mind that the timeframe can be adjusted if life events make the attainment too difficult. Simply adding a date will make a goal time-bound—*"I will start a carpool"* becomes *"I will start a carpool by the end of next week."*

> *"Experience is not the best teacher. Evaluated experience is."* —John C. Maxwell

SKILL NO. 4
GIVING FEEDBACK

The fourth skill is giving feedback. Did you know that more than half of workers get feedback less than one time per week?[25] Looking at managerial skills, three hundred heads of HR ranked giving feedback dead last.[26] Clearly we need to get better at this! Here are some things you can do:

Encouragement/Positive feedback

Positive feedback is an important aspect of self-efficacy, a person's belief in his or her ability to succeed in a particular situation.[27] Getting verbal encouragement from others helps people overcome self-doubt, allowing them to focus on giving their best effort to the task at hand.

Use the modes of encouragement that your mentee or mentor is most used to—email, text, Facebook, or even a handwritten note may all be appropriate way to give feedback. Other principles of feedback I have found to be helpful are:

• Ask/grant permission (feedback is better received if the recipient is prepared to receive it).
• Set expectations for how you like to receive feedback (when, where, how, etc.).
• Make it timely.
• Make it sincere.
• Be clear and direct.

• Be specific.
> -**Nice:** "You are a great presenter."
> -**Better:** "The presentation you gave was well-organized."
> -**Best:** "I thought your presentation was effective because you used colorful illustrations, you gave practical examples, and you finished with strong recommendations.

The more specific you are, the more easily people know what it is they did well and what they can do differently to continue to grow.

IN ACTION

CORRECTIVE FEEDBACK NEEDED

Jamie was a young, inexperienced guy but with a great enthusiasm that made him a likeable entry-level hire. The assumption was that because he was younger, he would naturally be more savvy on the computer and could handle administrative duties easily. Unfortunately, this assumption almost became the undoing of the organization as electronic files were irretrievably lost, spreadsheets were rendered inaccurate, and critical notes miscommunicated. Even through corrective feedback and development plans, Jamie was unable to get to the skill level needed. As likeable as he was, Jamie was let go.

Six months later, Jamie saw his ex-boss in a social setting. Jamie, to his credit, walked up to her and thanked her for upholding the high standards of the organization by letting him go. He told her that it forced him to look at his life, what he really enjoyed, and what he wanted to do for work. He had just finished training as a massage therapist and was happier than ever.

Corrective feedback

Use the above guidelines for giving feedback along with the following:
• Focus on improving performance and on the future.
• Comment on behavior, not personality or character.
• Avoid using absolute language like "always" or "never."
• Focus on performance over which the person receiving the feedback has control.

Personal touch

Show you are behind them now, just as they are, but that you care enough not to let them stay there. Tell them specifically why you believe in them and their capabilities. Let them know that you see great things in their future.

SKILL NO. 5
INSPIRING

The final basic mentoring skill is "inspiring." You can never underestimate the importance of inspiration for both the mentor and the mentee. Inspiring ignites passion, and passion is the fuel that propels people forward. Share stories. Celebrate vision.

Discuss successes and what you did to achieve them. Talk about challenges you've had and what you did to overcome them.

> *"Never underestimate the power of dreams and the influence of the human spirit. We are all the same in the notion. The potential for greatness lives within each of us."*
> *—Wilma Rudolph*

For the mentee: Inspire your mentors with your passion to grow, to make a difference, to find your purpose, to move forward in the organization—whatever you hope to gain through the mentoring relationship. Your mentors need to see that you are ready, motivated, and will not waste their time. As you inspire them, they will up their game, knowing what they do and how they work with you really matters. Both of you win.

For the mentor: Growth is a difficult thing. Hard work and periodic setbacks can take a toll on your mentees' motivation. Telling inspirational stories, particularly about how you may have failed but kept on going, can give your mentees a boost. Be specific about why you believe in them and inspire them with a vision of their successful future. Challenge them to dream bigger and you will help them reach heights they would not have thought possible on their own.

SECTION 1
BEST PRACTICES

Mentee-run relationships: In counseling, the success of creating life change is attributable to 40% readiness of the counselee, 40% motivation of the counselee, and only 20% skill of the counselor. I believe this translates well to the mentoring relationship. If the mentee is not ready or motivated to change and grow, there isn't much that a mentor can do.

Keep it simple: Mentoring as a relational strategy is effective in an uncomplicated structure. Keep the evaluation process simple and nimble so that it is fluid and effective. Check the basic transfer of learning. Are mentees able to discuss changes they are implementing in their lives? Discuss reasons for why or why not. Show them this is the path to change.

Asking questions versus giving advice: Surprisingly (especially for those who like control) you are a more effective mentor when you have less control of the process, because then spontaneity and authenticity can take over. Mentors should ask open-ended, challenging questions rather than offering advice upfront. Teach how to think and reason through issues, not what to think and do.

Use questions like: "What do you think would be a strategic way to work through this? How do you think this should be handled? What do you think your options are? What additional information might you need? Is there a better way to go about this that has not really been considered?" You don't need to know all the answers. You may know basic ideas, but your mentee knows how to apply them to his or her personal situation.

Allow for time: Mentoring is a process, not an outcome, and it takes time. Interestingly, students who had intermittent mentoring relationships did worse than those who had no mentoring at all.[28] So, however it is set up, mentoring needs to be enough of a long-term relationship that there is time and accountability to support growth.

More than one: Establish a web of mentoring relationships. As we've already discussed, team mentoring works well in difficult economic times. Web mentoring helps create a mentoring culture where everyone wins, because everyone is learning from multiple sources. Consider being mentored by a subordinate instead of the reverse. Watch the dynamics of what happens. What did you learn? What was most valuable about the experience? View multiple people as sources for impactful learning.

Think of entry level outside your organization: Use mentoring for creating interest in your organization. Pair university students with people already in the workplace. This is a great strategy for recruiting—it cuts recruiting costs, streamlines efforts, and helps new hires acclimate much more quickly. Some organizations intentionally locate their offices close to educational institutions for just this reason (e.g., Google has an office close to the University of Michigan).

KEY POINTS/HIGHLIGHTS

- Mentoring is not complicated. It is a very powerful tool for change.

- Mentoring is effective for developing individuals and organizations. It encourages employee engagement and organizational productivity.

- Research supports numerous benefits that mentoring provides to mentors, mentees, and organizations.

- Mentoring is most effective when a mentoring culture is encouraged, utilizing both formal and informal mentoring models.

- Certain characteristics make mentors, mentees, and mentoring relationships most effective.

- There are four basic steps to a mentoring relationship:
  1. Establishing processes and expectations
  2. Building the relationship
  3. Developing the mentee
  4. Evaluation/celebration/recommendations

- There are five skills that, if understood and performed well, will promote a healthy and productive mentoring relationship:
  -Listening
  -Building trust
  -Establishing goals
  -Giving feedback
  -Inspiring

SO WHAT !

WHY THIS WILL MAKE A DIFFERENCE IN YOUR ORGANIZATION

Mentoring is a key strategy for employee development in organizations. It is simple, uses current resources, and most people can be trained in it very easily. Mentoring is a wise training vehicle in times of economic downturn.

The benefits for supporting a mentoring program are numerous, affecting employee engagement, productivity, knowledge transfer and growth, communication, recruiting, retention, succession, brand identity, and diversity. Mentoring is a strong tool for harnessing passion and moving toward organizational vision. Formal mentoring programs encourage development of employees and ultimately organizations. A mentoring culture (which includes formal and informal mentoring) encourages exponential growth and helps in contextualizing learning for organizational gains.

TAKING IT FORWARD

Take time to write down any reflections, points to remember, or next steps that you will take forward as a result of what you have considered while reading this chapter.

_____

_____

_____

_____

_____

_____

_____

_____

_____

_____

SECTION 1
EXERCISES

1. MENTORING—PAST INSIGHTS: (fill out and then discuss with mentor/mentee)

Describe a successful mentoring relationship you experienced.

_____

_____

Describe a mentoring relationship that did not work out well.

_____

_____

Based on your evaluation of the above relationships, what characteristics of a mentoring relationship matter most to you?

_____

_____

Gauge growth: When was the last time you did something you haven't done before? What learning have you applied in the last few months? How might you increase these opportunities in the future? How might they be supported in a mentoring relationship?

_____

_____

_____

_____

2. MENTORING EXPECTATIONS:

How often, when, and where will we meet? How long will the relationship last?

Limits or constraints that may affect our meeting and how we'll handle these:

What do I hope to learn from you? How can we get the most from each other?

How will we give each other feedback, both positive and corrective (In person? Written? Immediate? Wait for one day? etc.):

How will we handle confidentiality (everything is okay to discuss unless specified, or nothing is okay to discuss unless specified):

Challenges we may face and how we'll address them:

Areas of growth I'd like to pursue (see "Choosing compelling direction" exercise below for help here):

Objectives/Goals we may work on:

Signed mentee _____

Signed mentor _____

3. PRACTICE LISTENING: Pair up with someone (preferably your mentor or mentee). Each of you will describe a childhood memory for five minutes (setting a timer is a good idea). The listener must only listen, affirm what is said, ask clarifying questions, but add no new information to the conversation ("I had a similar experience…" is off-limits!). After the time is up, switch roles of listener and storyteller.

What did you like about being the listener? The one listened to?

Being a listener: _____

_____

_____

Being listened to: _____

_____

_____

What did you not like or what frustrated you?

Being a listener: _____

_____

_____

Being listened to: _____

_____

_____

How can you use what you learned in this exercise in the future?

_____

_____

4. PRACTICE BEING CURIOUS: Keep a tally of how many questions you ask versus pieces of information you give in a single day. Make a goal to ask two questions for every piece of information you give.

Number of questions asked: _____

Number of pieces of information given: _____

5. BUILDING TRUST: Building trust is critical to a productive mentoring relationship. List below the things that would help build trust in your relationships. Then list what would break trust in your relationships. Share these with your mentee/mentor.

Trust Builders	Trust Busters
_____	_____
_____	_____
_____	_____
_____	_____
_____	_____
_____	_____

6. CHOOSING COMPELLING DIRECTION: Here are questions you might ask your mentee that will help generate ideas for meaningful goals.

• What skills would you like to develop? Is there a career path you are pursuing but will need to have training or education prior to advancing any further? What steps do you need to take to reach your desired position?

• Provoke an outlandish idea. In your wildest dreams, what would you want people to say about you? If you were completely confident, what would you do?

• If you never had to worry about another bill or finances, what would you do with your life? How can you bring those passions into your work?

• What problems need to be solved? How can you contribute to the solution? How will your life be different if these problems are solved?

• What steps do you need to take to have a more integrated personal and work life? How might you need to relax and refuel?

• Observe which skills/strengths the mentee has that the organization is not currently using well or at all. Which aspects of his/her current projects does he/she enjoy most? What strengths could you encourage the mentee to increase based on these observations?

SMART Goal Setting Practice: For the following statements, change the goal so that it reflects the word in **bold**. For example:

Specific: I want to be more educated.
<u>I want to learn how to speak French fluently.</u>

Specific: I want to raise good kids.

_____

Measurable: I will become a better writer.

_____

Achievable: I will lose 30 pounds this week.

_____

Relevant: I will send CD players to tsunami survivors in India.

_____

Time-bound: I will sign up for a class on effective briefings.

_____

I want to be a better person (Write a meaningful goal that fits the SMART criteria):

_____

7. GIVING FEEDBACK: Consider the two scenarios below. How would you give feedback that is s clear, direct, honest, specific and behavior-focused?

Scenario 1:
You just observed your mentee conduct a meeting. Overall the meeting went well and people left with clear next steps on what they were to do. On two occasions, however, your mentee lost control of the meeting. Imagine why this might have happened and give feedback below.

Feedback:

_____
_____
_____
_____

Scenario 2:
Your mentee/mentor has broken confidentiality and shared a story you told, specifics and all. You thought you'd been very clear that the story needed to stay between the two of you due to its potential to cause others to think less of you without knowing all the details. You suspect the reason the story was shared was because it affected your mentee/mentor deeply.

Feedback:

_____
_____
_____
_____

8. INSPIRING: What stories might you share with a mentee that would be inspirational? Think specifically about times you failed or things didn't go as planned, but you didn't let it stop you.

1. _____
_____
_____
_____
_____
_____

2. _____
_____
_____
_____
_____
_____

What stories have you heard recently that have inspired you? What about these stories inspired you?

1. Story: _____
_____
_____
_____
_____

What specifically made this inspiring? _____

_____

_____

_____

How might you use this idea to inspire others?

_____

_____

_____

2. Story: _____

_____

_____

_____

_____

What specifically made this inspiring? _____

_____

_____

_____

How might you use this idea to inspire others?

_____

_____

_____

SECTION 2

MENTORING THROUGH DIFFERENCES

WHAT YOU NEED TO KNOW ABOUT MENTORING WITH PEOPLE WHO ARE DIFFERENT THAN YOU (WHICH IS PRETTY MUCH EVERYONE!)

A 2008 study by Noble Business Solutions reports that the internal challenges businesses experience have to do with human resources more than corporate systems—motivation, developing the next generation of leaders, the sense of team, and other human capital issues. They also assert that having a great, positive team is a huge competitive advantage since people issues so often get in the way of forward progress.[29] I have found that employees leave their jobs because of people issues more than because of specific job tasks.

Differences between people are often an impetus for human resource issues. The sooner you embrace differences, the sooner you can move forward together with others.

 **IN ACTION**

NO ONE WANTS OATMEAL EVERY DAY

When I was younger, vegetables never appealed to me. Anything green would automatically receive a curled lip. Now I'm hard-pressed to find a vegetable I don't like. Please know, I am not equating the intricacies of human relationships with food dislikes, but I think there is an analogy here. Really great dishes are composed of many ingre dients. It is how they work together that brings out new culinary delights. In fact, the hottest new trends in cooking are to combine foods that would not normally wind up in the same dish: Asian sweet chili with Italian cheeses, chocolate with beef, or cauliflower with dessert. There are really no "wrong" foods (except the ones that may bring on a severe allergy), and there are really no foods which are always "right" (although I could make an argument for tree-ripened peaches sliced generously over homemade ice cream). It is all a matter of perspective, experience, personal taste, and upbringing.

The people we come in contact with can be ingredients to an amazing organizational "dish." Too much of one ingredient or perspective can become too much of the same thing. Like plain oatmeal—bland and boring. Diversity in a group allows for new creations, innovations, tastes, and ideas we have not yet come across. Developing a genuine sense of curiosity rather than settling back into a judgmental stance can make all the difference in helping us appreciate diversity. I would not look at another person eating okra (the one vegetable I am not fond of) and think they are "wrong" to do so. I often wonder—with a genuine sense of curiosity—what they taste in it that makes them enjoy it. If we can look at the opinions and perspectives of others in the same curious manner—"I wonder what makes them feel or think that way?"—it will help us take on an accepting and respectful stance instead of a combative one. Then creativity and innovation can begin.

One of the best ways to begin is to be authentic—don't be afraid to show genuine passion for what is important to you. This can be a point of contact with others who may not be like you. We all have basic needs, wants, and values. You can find commonalities in the broader categories even if the specific ways you live your life seems odd to others. Most people want to be successful, to be loved, to make a difference, to be profitable. This doesn't mean that you have to throw out your standards just to get along. Acceptance is not necessarily an endorsement—you don't have to agree with everything someone does in order to value them as a person.

> *"The task of leadership is not to put greatness into people, but to elicit it, for the greatness is there already." —John Buchan*

As I've said before, how differences are handled in your organization sends a clear message to your employees regarding how they are valued for their unique contributions. Mentoring is the strongest way to work through the differences that may cause problems or distract from accomplishing the business of the day. Mentoring builds bridges between people. The connections fostered through mentoring relationships promote mutual tolerance and appreciation. Other people are no longer just strangers, but rather people into whom you have invested time and effort. You have come to know them on a personal level, and have begun to build mutual respect, thereby short-circuiting divisiveness. The result is that your organizations can benefit from the diversity in your employees, using the differences to work synergistically, promoting a safe place for creative thought, and spurring innovation as varied perspectives are honored, listened to, and acted upon.

SECTION 2
BEST PRACTICES

Get away from debates about right and wrong

People have differing perspectives—one perspective need not be proved wrong to value another. Negative judgments stifle people, which in turn choke the organization's forward movement. So rather than posturing to be "right," foster a genuine curiosity and desire for understanding. The result will be a respectful work environment that not only recognizes all aspects of its human resources, but also makes the best use of them.

When you feel yourself getting irritated with how other people are going about tasks at work or how they contribute to discussions, or how they approach the past, or how they approach their work day, examine that feeling. Irritation is not helpful, ever. Not for you, not for communicating clearly, not for working though and expressing ideas, not for creativity, not for innovation. As mentioned above, step back and take on a curious stance. Wonder—what makes them approach things that way? What can you learn? What about their perspective might be needed?

> *"I note the obvious differences between each sort and type, but we are more alike, my friends, than we are unalike."*
> —Maya Angelou

Avoid blame

Blame stunts creativity and makes people afraid to take risks. People often use blame to take the negative spotlight off themselves, shifting responsibility for mistakes to someone else. But if you can feel keen responsibility for the end results rather than for the small steps along the way, it will be easier to resist the blame game. Instead, you can use that energy to keep moving toward your organizational goals. Rather than getting embroiled in a destructive cycle of blame, you will be free to be inventive. Finding fault looks backward—creating looks forward. Viewing others' unique contributions without negative or positive undertones allows you to learn from the things that don't work. They simply become things you know not to repeat in the future.

Releasing the desire to blame means believing in the best intentions from those you work with. If you have established good working relationships with these people through formal or informal mentoring, this belief comes more easily.

> *"What we see depends on what we look for."*
> *—John Lubbock*

Believe the best

Begin every interaction with respect for other people and the belief that they are trying to do their best. Remind yourself that their goal is not to be frustrating—they are acting from a place that makes sense to them. Assuming the best lays the groundwork for differences to be celebrated rather than scrutinized. Employees will have a safer place to exercise their unique strengths without feeling tethered. This can only strengthen the human assets of your organization.

Lay it on the line

When a fellow worker irritates you, ask "Why am I so bothered by this?" Consider whether it's something that is a good reason for frustration, or if instead just a different way of doing things than you are familiar with. If it is the latter, try to see what you might learn from the different perspective.

If it is the former, mention it with respect. People won't know how they are coming off unless you tell them. Don't be afraid to say what needs to be said, but affirm them in the process. For instance, you could say, "I know you mean well, but when you said that to me it seemed like you were talking down to me." Or, "I know you are excited about this project, but when you move forward without regard for others' opinions, it comes across as arrogant."

Address negative comments about differences quickly. This will actually reinforce the relationship and encourage further honesty and risk. The issue is rarely the issue; the real problem is often control. If you can loosen your grip on trying to control every situation, you will be more open to new ideas and foster an environment that encourages innovation.

The easy way out?

Best practices for dealing with differences among the people in your organization do not necessarily involve making things "easier." Easier can't be the ultimate goal, but helping people engage should be. Invite discussion of next steps rather than assuming that others will simply agree with the steps you want to implement. If everyone owns the solution and believes that all contributions matter, the solutions will be more robust and more resistant to derailment.

> *"Flatter me, and I may not believe you. Criticize me, and I may not like you. Ignore me, and I may not forgive you. Encourage me, and I will not forget you." —William Arthur Ward*

Encourage confidence

Help the people in your organization find competence and credibility. Be willing to put a diverse group in high-trust positions to avoid the "yes man" syndrome. Openly and publicly give people approval for ideas and actions that contribute to the bottom line. Openly endorse their innovative ideas, even if they go against things as they have been in the past. Show that creativity is encouraged rather than stifled. The forward traction created by this type of encouragement can propel your organization forward to places you may not have predicted, but will be diverse enough to allow you to nimbly address the demands of your rapidly changing business environments.

It's contagious!

Motivation begets motivation—it is positively contagious. Capture each other's interest by active listening, cast a vision of a compelling future, nurture passion, and cultivate strengths. The positive energy produced will sustain the organization when things get difficult.

> *"If your actions inspire others to dream more, do more, and become more, you are a leader."* —John Quincy Adams

Take time to go deep

Take advantage of multiple perspectives. Set aside time for creativity, problem solving, and conflict management among diverse groups within your organization. Allowing for diverse perspectives to be heard takes time, but it is worth it to take conversations to a deeper level. Your solutions will be less superficial, addressing more diversity in thought and creative options.

Agree on disagreement

Help your mentees build bridges through conflict rather than allowing it to separate them from others. Interestingly, a person who is resistant is more committed to the organization than someone who is merely compliant because resistance requires engagement. So, don't be afraid to provoke and model disagreement. You can have meaningful conversations about what happened later in order to deepen the relationships. This will add value to each person, and again allow for conflict to spur conversation rather than derail it.

Moving into the 3G's

We have been looking at how to best work with the differences among the people in our organizations. The remainder of this book will examine three types of differences that organizations may deal with:

• Generational Distinctions
• Global Diversity
• Gender Differences

Your organization may be struggling with challenges posed by one of the above, or even all three. We have found that it is best to work proactively with these differences so they become springboards for creativity rather than cause for conflict.

The two methodologies that work well in my experience are:

• **Education** about what the differences really are and where they come from.

• **Establishing mentoring relationships** to help work through the challenges often posed by these differences.

The next part of this book includes three sections which will address each of these issues in turn. We'll examine what these differences look like, why they exist, best practices for working with them, and exercises to promote unity (but not homogeneity) within all three types.

KEY POINTS/HIGHLIGHTS

- How differences are handled will speak to how people are valued in your organization.

- Differences can be synergistic.

- Embrace commonalities.

- Move away from right/wrong and blame.

- Believe the best.

- Identify sources of irritation.

- Agree to disagree.

- Understand the key to working with differences: Education about what makes people different and how to establish mentoring relationships to help work through the challenges posed by these differences.

SO WHAT !

WHY THIS WILL MAKE A DIFFERENCE IN YOUR ORGANIZATION

Becoming aware of differences, understanding why people act differently than you would, and appreciating diversity with curiosity instead of criticism is critical to current business strategy. Refrain from stereotyping and judging—instead see that differences do not need to be threatening, they are just different.

Mentoring can bridge these differences by developing respect and understanding through relationships. It promotes a learning culture (especially when informal mentoring is encouraged) where differences are seen as an avenue for exponential learning, resulting in creativity and growth that appreciating differences fosters. When diversity is celebrated, destructive conflict is discouraged. This keeps positive momentum on track. Different perspectives can create synergies that are not possible with homogeneous "group think." The resulting increase in creativity and practical innovation is a strong path to a competitive edge in today's rapidly changing marketplace.

TAKING IT FORWARD

Take time to write down any reflections, points to remember, or next steps that you will take forward as a result of what you have considered while reading this chapter.

_____

_____

_____

_____

_____

_____

_____

"If I were to wish for anything, I should not wish for wealth and power, but for the passionate sense of the potential, for the eye which, ever young and ardent, sees the possible. Pleasure disappoints, possibility never." —Søren Kierkegaard

SECTION 2
EXERCISES

1. EMPLOY THE NEGATIVITY POLICE: Discourage complaining and make it clear that it is not a mode of conversation that is promoted in your organization. Strip negativity from your vocabulary, and model this for others. Heighten your awareness of negativity and refuse to allow it to be a part of what you do. There is no upside to negativity; it only pulls people down and stifles momentum.

2. PUT RESOURCES ON DIVERSITY HYPER-DRIVE: Utilize internal learning websites, logs, and lists of resources. Make them robust and based on the best information available. Make sure you are taking advantage of the diversity in your organization through this type of information share. Include provocative questions to elicit diverse perspectives, knowledge, and best practices.

Provide deeper training on more complex skills like building trust, gauging and taking risks, promoting motivation, expanding areas of strength, and character development. This type of training will help sustain vision and motivation in difficult times more than simple skill development will.

3. BUILD A TRUST CULTURE: Consider the issue of trust—whom do you trust and why? How did you build that trust? Whose trust is important to you? Why? What have been trust busters in your experience? What guidelines can you and your team decide on that would build a trusting organizational culture? What has hurt this effort in the past? How can you repair trust if it has been violated? How can you avoid future pitfalls? Write a trust agreement that everyone can sign.

4. ENGAGE YOUR NETWORK: Examine your leadership network: (Both those whom you lead, and those who lead you). Whom do you trust? Who trusts you? Who challenges you? What types of people do you like to lead? What types of people do you like to be led by? How can you bring diversity to your network? In-depth self-examination like this may shed light on areas in which your connections have become too homogeneous. Consider mentoring or being mentored as a way to expand the diversity of your relationships and leadership.

5. LOOK FOR COMMONALITY, NOT DIVISION: What core values do you and those in your organization share? What areas of commonality can you embrace? Brainstorm and discuss any differences you have and where they may come from.

Share some of your personal story with each other. This will help you find commonalities you may have not known existed. Things like heroes, family, hobbies, significant past events, successes, and hard times.

Discuss topics where everyone will most likely have an opinion, like "The top 10 common career mistakes people make" or "How to work with difficult people." What common themes emerge? What differences? Finding commonality will help balance areas of diversity, keeping people from categorizing others in terms of "completely right" or "completely wrong".

6. MIX IT UP: In group meetings, assign seats and mix groups up to make them more diverse (e.g., different levels in the organization, different generational representation, different personalities). Rotate leadership in these groups. Incorporate training and support of diverse leaders into your corporate culture. These types of actions show that diversity is respected and encouraged.

3

PART TWO

G

THE THREE G'S

SECTION 3

THE FOUR GENERATIONS IN THE WORKFORCE

"THAT WHICH SEEMS THE HEIGHT OF ABSURDITY IN ONE GENERATION OFTEN BECOMES THE HEIGHT OF WISDOM IN ANOTHER." —ADLAI STEVENSON

"I mean really...she seems to not even care or be interested in what we are doing..."

"All he seems to care about is structure and rules...what about creativity outside the lines?"

"It drives me nuts...He sits around like he is entitled to have people take care of him..."

"Why does everyone just assume that the boss is "right"...I have to admit I have concerns..."

"How can they move forward in business with such blatant disregard for the harm they are doing to the environment?"

"Why does she feel she has to stay at one business her whole life? I would die of boredom."

These are just a few examples of the growing misunderstanding and intolerance that often exists among the four generations currently represented in the workplace. Each of these generations is marked by attitudes, perspectives, values, and motivations that have been shaped by social and global events particular to them. The differences experienced between each generation can be divisive when they aren't understood more completely.

A study by Noble Business Solutions in 2008 found that generational issues were most concerning to organizations because of the high turnover rate they cause. Turnover costs can easily range from 50% to 150% of an employee's salary,[30] so retaining talented and competent people translates into a competitive advantage. Retaining key talent at Sysco Corporation saved nearly $50 million in hiring and training costs for new associates.[31] Employee engagement (feeling tied to corporate vision, and feeling they are a part of that vision being accomplished) is also relevant to business bottom lines. For example, Best Buy Corporation found $100,000 value in a single store with an increase of just 0.1% in employee engagement.[32]

> *"Those of us who are older tend to underestimate the difference between generations. We think that what feels comfortable to us will not—or should not—be a barrier to those who are younger. Those of us who are younger tend to over-estimate the difference between generations."[33] —John Ortberg*

If people can stop complaining and start championing all the generations, important alliances can form which will help organizations move forward. Actions speak loudly, and lip service to diversity does little without visible steps toward respecting, encouraging, and promoting that diversity. Do you come from a place of frustration or instead can you come from a place of mutual esteem? Remember as you work on building relationships, that you will often find strong commonalities in wanting to be valued, having a purpose, doing a good job, and desiring opportunities to learn and grow. Finding these commonalities goes a long way to reduce frustration and increase respect.

As we've seen, people who know, like, and respect each other are much more productive overall than those who lack respect and camaraderie. Most people want to be accepted where they are, not where other people think they should be. They'd like to see a clear path to clear goals. They want others to assume they are doing their best, the offer of compassion and patience during the learning process, support as they take risks, and a soft place to land when they fall. We've also seen that informal and formal mentoring is a strong method for organizations to create these relationships that can bridge across differences. Let's take a bird's-eye view the generational distinctions in today's workplace before diving in.

MILLENNIALS VS. BOOMERS

If you look at recently published business articles and books, you'll see that the youngest generation, the Millennials, is causing consternation in the work world. Other generations perceive this group to be entitled, unwilling to work, and ready to quit without provocation.

But what may be seen as entitlement may actually be disappointment and frustration in disguise. Millennials have been told their whole lives that they could do anything, be anything, have anything, and that a college education would yield a job that would pay well and satisfy. What they are finding, however, is that the workplace is not as hospitable as their homes have been. The voices that their parents cultivated in them are not honored, respected, nor asked for in the workplace. There is the expectation that dues must be paid—after all, the Baby Boomers and Traditionalists had to pay them. These older generations may be operating out of a sense of fairness, but to the Millennials, it feels like a bunch of unnecessary rules and irrelevant hoops to jump through. So they feel stifled and disrespected.

Other generations may think that Millennials should consider substituting their frustration and anger in favor of doing the best possible job with a great attitude in even the most menial of tasks. I agree that it would give a base of respect and is a place to start, but this may not be the most effective long-term solution. What do organizations miss by not giving Millennials the opportunity to voice their perspectives and ideas?

David Wraight, author of *The Next Wave*, believes that the "empowerment response" is most effective with the younger, globally-connected generation. He believes we need to see them as people who can lead us, who have important skills and knowledge to share. They don't require titles or positions to feel like they have influence. They are activists, cause creators, and leaders. They want to be proud of the companies they work for.

Jeffrey Arnett, respected scholar of young adults, sees the group as possessing five main characteristics:

1. They are exploring their identities in love and work.
2. They are self-focused.
3. They are at an age of instability.
4. They see life as full of endless possibilities for work, relationships, and where they may live, and they love to explore as many as they can.
5. They see themselves existing in the gap between adolescence and adulthood.[34]

> *"We don't see things as they are, we see things as we are"* —Anais Nin

Unfortunately, Millennials are often structurally disconnected in organizations and socially cut off from older adults who could be mentors. And yet, mentoring can legitimize Millennials and bring out their best. It can build bridges and connect them to other generations that don't often cross in natural social circles. Although there are programs for developing skills in young leaders, mentoring offers these younger generations a way into the tight leadership circles that are dominated by the Baby Boomer generation. With mentoring, Millennials are more likely to advance, to earn more, enjoy their work more, and more clearly define their vision and future goals. And as the Baby Boomers begin to retire in droves, empowering Millennials now will ensure that they will become the largest talent and leadership pool to replace them.

Regrettably, there exists a real lack of training and mentoring as Boomers hold tightly to their positions, having been brought up in a highly competitive environment where power is a zero-sum game. Add to this the fact that the failing economy has made it impossible for older workers to retire, which has increased their resentment and fight to remain in control. Even when the Boomers do leave, their positions have been marked by much time and sacrifice and very little fun, which is not very appealing to the younger generations. So the transition of leadership, power, and job function has become disjointed at best.

Generation X sandwich

And what about Generation X? They also have a reputation for being negative and for leaving corporations to become entrepreneurs. In their defense, they are sandwiched between the larger generations of Boomers and Millennials and feel unappreciated, disillusioned with corporate corruption, and that they are just there to hold the place between Baby Boomer retirement and Millennials getting up to speed.

So what can be done?

Younger generations want to learn from older ones, to be respected for their contributions, and to enjoy shared power. Older generations want their legacy to be recognized, and feel they are still viable and relevant. So what can be done with generational differences at work? Conflicting expectations get in the way, and yet each generation has much to offer. Let's take a look at what makes each of the generations tick (keeping in mind these are generalizations, and that people on one end or the other of a generational group may take one or more characteristics of the next generation, as well).

> *"It is not just that each generation learns from each other, but also that there is an electricity present due to the coming together of so many great yet various hearts and minds."*
> —Lisa Haneberg, Coaching Up and Down the Generations

THE FOUR GENERATIONS IN THE WORKPLACE

TRADITIONALISTS
Born: 1922–1945
55 million, 10% of current workforce

• **Events:** This is "The Silent Generation," which lived through World War II and the Korean War. They saw the rise of unions, the GI Bill, film and projectors, suburbia, and AM radio. For them, blackboards, handwritten correspondence, landlines, rotary dials, and typewriters were the norm. They saw the stock market crash, the Depression, the Bomb, and the beginning of jazz.

• **Values:** Tradition, loyalty, structure, hard work, doing one's duty, and thriftiness are most important. They believe that your word is your bond; they are motivated by a job well done, and are linear in thought.

• **Retirement:** They are mostly retired, but looking for things to supplement their income. They are in good health but have economic uncertainties due to fixed incomes and a questionable economy. They want to still contribute in a meaningful way.

• **Legacy:** Their vast knowledge and wisdom are lost when they leave. So retaining their legacy through relationships is critical.

• **Attitudes:** They are patient, used to delayed gratification, and working longer for something.

• **Mentoring:** They make excellent mentors, particularly for Millennials, because they are far enough away from the Millennial's parents' generation. Millennials respect traditionalists in a way that even Boomers don't.

BABY BOOMERS
Born: 1946–64
84 million, 44% of current workforce

• **Events:** They lived through the Cold War, the Vietnam War, JFK and MLK (and their assassinations), the military draft, the sexual revolution, and the women's and civil rights movements. They saw the rise of television, rock-and-roll, tape recorders, 8-track tapes, and the Beatles. They generated the "Me" decade of the 1970s and the relentless pursuit of wealth in the 1980s.

• **Value:** They work to get ahead and focus on competition and success. They are motivated by symbols of success like titles, corner offices, and promotions. It's not just a job or career, it's their life. They want to put their stamp on things, not simply do the job.

• **Attitudes:** They are optimistic, competitive, and driven by success.

• **Longevity:** Growing old is a stigma for this generation, and they are relentless in their pursuit to reclaim youth. The soft job market and economic crisis has found many Boomers taking jobs for which they feel over-qualified. They want to stay involved in creative ways and still work if they retire, but many can't retire yet because they still need a high income to sustain the lifestyle to which they have become accustomed. They are less flexible and become more concrete as they grow older.

• **Concerns:** They are sandwiched between caring for kids and parents. This contributes to retirement worries because they still have dependents in two generations.

• **Authority:** They have a love-hate relationship with authority. They respect hierarchies and paying dues, but they also have been shown to be willing to overturn unjust authority (e.g., civil rights, women's movement).

• **Thoughts on younger generations:** They often view Millennials as a threat to authority, to the "right way of doing things," to the hard work it has taken to pay dues, and the wisdom of life experience. As they get older, they tend not to be as open to new ideas and direction, and become more rigid.[35]

• **Competition:** Boomers had to compete for everything. The world was too small, and winning became a very big deal. Their fierce competitiveness led to longer work hours (adding one month of work hours per year!) to achieve the results they wanted.

GENERATION X
Born: 1965-1980
46 million, 34% of current workforce

• **Events:** They saw the Persian Gulf and the Challenger explosion, as well as recessions, corporate corruption, downsizing, and the tripling of the divorce rate. MTV, *X-Files*, answering machines, Apple 2, Atari, cable TV, car phones, CDs, the Internet, satellite TV, desktop publishing, VCRs and the computer revolution became influences. Race, gender, and sexual orientation were no longer strict identifiers as those lines became blurred.

• **Value:** Change, life balance, flexibility, self-discovery, and freedom are most important. They are motivated by regular feedback, learning, and informality. As realists, they are the first generation who did not expect to be more affluent than their parents. They watched their parents work themselves to death. After growing up as latch-key kids, they are tenacious about work/life balance and the rights of parents, which paved the way for the helicopter parenting (the constant hovering) the Millennials have embraced.

• **Distrust of corporate structures:** They feel a sense of alienation, skepticism, and economic anxiety. Security and safety can't be assumed or taken for granted and they need a climate of trust. They have an independent contractor mentality and see business as an ongoing game of musical chairs. Being a slave to a corporation is an empty endeavor. They have a strong value-orientation because they had to learn what really mattered.

• **Conflict:** Corporate restructuring and economic uncertainty have made them skeptical but escapists. They don't want to be talked down to or de-valued. They are used to people keeping their heads down to avoid conflict. However, push them too far and they will blow or leave.

• **Autonomy:** They don't love corporate America but are looking for ways to contribute and will get involved if a compelling offer comes up and they think they'll be valued. They need autonomy—just show them the path to promotion and leadership. Choices, goals, and deadlines are important to them and they want to be involved in the decision-making process. They typically reject conventional leadership norms because of the corruption they witnessed. As children of divorced parents, they often came home to empty houses and were expected to fend for themselves, so they are not bound by real or virtual boundaries.

• **Attitude toward Boomers and Millennials:** They see Boomers as egocentric—perceiving that Boomers think they are "the" generation. No one can compare because the Boomers' way is the only way. They think that Boomers won't retire. They are stuck at mid-level management and frustrated because they may feel like stand-ins as they train the Boomers' replacements (the Millennials) but are not the replacements themselves. Xers feel overlooked and unappreciated which leads them to start their own businesses and become entrepreneurial.

MILLENNIALS (GENERATION Y)
1981-2004
88 million, 10% of current workforce

Author's note: This section on Millennials is much longer and in-depth than those of the earlier generations. This extra analysis does not reflect a bias toward or against this generation. I have included it as is because there is so much currently being written on the Millennials due to the effect that their entrance into the work force and the large size of the generation will have. This is causing considerable debate on how best to encourage this generation and maximize its potential.

• **Events:** They witnessed Desert Storm, 9/11, and the resulting conflicts in the Middle East. They also saw the rise of social media, school violence, You Tube, AOL, broadband, cell phones, Facebook, Google, and IT.

• **Value:** They want informality, passion, creativity, and initiative.

• **Paying Dues:** They don't see the need or value of "paying your dues" or other rites of passage. They don't believe that they aren't old enough, experienced enough, educated enough, or don't have the qualifications needed. Things change fast and Millennials quickly evaluate whether something makes sense or fits their life because of this, and they aren't afraid to voice their opinion.

• **Parents:** They have had extremely accommodating parents. In fact, their most trusted friends are their parents. Interestingly, they share their parents' values in support of the importance of home, family, and community. They are sheltered and conventional, and their parents wanted them (as evidenced by the quadrupling of infertility visits in late 80s). A significantly higher number (than other generations), 25% were raised in a single-parent home which may affect how they view traditional parental roles. They have been training their parents in technology and social media, resulting in role reversal. This generation of wanted children became central to their parent's sense of purpose. Their well-being has dominated legislation with unheard of new law regulating things like child restraints, home products, and video game ratings.

• **Attitude:** About 90% of Millennials describe themselves as happy, confident and positive[36] in contrast to the Xers, who have a more pessimistic stance. They combine the hopefulness of the Boomers with the conviction of Generation X. They are a by-product of the self-esteem movement of the 80s and their optimism is a positive attribute, but can sometimes create unrealistic goals and expectations. They expect things to happen quickly and multi-sensory. They are used to multi-tasking and have a limited attention span. They grew up with TV shows where any problem was fixed in sixty minutes or less. They are optimistic and idealistic, with a deep desire to make their mark in the world. They do not want to just observe—they want to be players in what is going on. They like winning and think it is always possible—gaming has let them believe that if they lose they just start over or change the rules.

• **Dealing with Diversity:** They have greater tolerance for people who are different from them because diversity is so common in their experience. They are also the most globally aware.

• **Comfort with Change:** Millennials thrive in an atmosphere of change because then they can put their mark on the future. They appreciate things that are relevant, current, fitting, and flexible. They are not afraid of change and innovation. They rebel not by being worse, but by being better. They are not afraid to tear down the old way of doing things if they aren't working or if they are corrupt. They are bored if there is nothing to do and will tune out if not interested. They are heavily programmed and impatient, expecting instant gratification and immediate feedback.

• **Group Affinity:** Having grown up doing everything in groups, they've learned that if the group wins, they win. Unfortunately, the ability to work in groups often masks their fear of making bad decisions on their own. They want to be surrounded by bright, creative people. They are tribal—more interested in connections than things. They are not a crowd, but rather a group with purpose waiting to be turned into movements. With such comfort with and focus on collective action, taking a solo leadership position is not necessarily valued.

• **Relationships:** Millennials rank "cementing relationships with colleagues and supervisors" as their number one challenge.[37] As we've already seen, relationships are paramount. If good connections aren't formed, they can suffer from great loneliness. Often the way they go about finding relationships is stunted by trying to decide what is real and what isn't in social media and other electronic relationship builders. Gender and race are non-issues, and they have friends from a variety of economic and ethnic backgrounds. They are willing to accept authority, and are open to being managed and taking direction. They desperately want mentors and actually want to have intergenerational relationships, but only with those seen as worthy of respect. Conversations with friends and then parents are the top two influences that shape decisions.[38]   Their strong loyalty to friends results from being in constant contact with their peers through social media and texting.

• **Need for Feedback:** They are high maintenance, high performers. They expect a lot from their jobs and from themselves. As attention sponges, they want constant feedback, praise, and recognition. They can be high maintenance, but they are also quite capable and savvy.

• **Making a Difference Matters:** They value making a difference, and are motivated by social justice. They look for work that is challenging and cause conscious. Up to 77% of Millennials believe the social aspects of work are "very important" to their overall sense of workplace satisfaction.[39]   So issues like being green and environmentally-conscious matter to them. They believe the best is possible and are hopeful—they are not afraid to work hard on something they believe in. Socially responsible, they take up volunteering and are against selfish consuming. They desire to be globally responsible and will get behind what they believe in.

• **Information:** With all the information in the world at their fingertips, Millennials need a trusted authority to help them filter it all. They are very comfortable with sound bytes. In fact, they expect information to be quick, easy to find, and don't want to take the time to verify the truth, so they are often duped. They desire a moral compass to point them to what information matters and what doesn't and they want trusted knowledge sources rather than the right answers to be handed to them. To avoid depression from information overload, this generation needs to know how their knowledge fits into their *particular* context.

> *"Technology is technology only for people who are born before it was invented."* —Alan Kay

• **Conflict:** When there is a conflict, Millennials will default to the group. They'll solicit other's opinions before dealing with a problem, and then they'll confront the offender head on. They love talking things out even if talking things out is done via texting on their phones.

• **Work:** The things Millennials look for in an employer is a company that will develop their skills for the future, has strong values, offers customizable options in a benefits/reward package, allows them to blend work with the rest of their life, and offers a clear career path.[40] Since they see life as quite integrated, they care about the kind of work they do—what is work and what is personal aren't separated. They want to change the world, but need a leader to show them why and how. They don't like to be put in a box with set parameters or being told how or when to do things. They want bosses who are comfortable with flexibility in schedule and environment. They need and value trusted relationships and are accepting but often not accepted. The balance between work and life is about working smarter so that less time is required.

• **Structure:** They are intuitive and go on "gut" feeling and street smarts. Structure frustrates them and they don't like to do things in a prescriptive way, and yet they appreciate structure if it gives them direction to move forward. They don't know where they will be in six months, so they are hesitant to commit. They are non-linear and literate in visual and multi-media forms. They expect to be able to control things anytime and anywhere because they are used to the customization they have experienced in software applications.

They challenge existing boundaries if they don't understand the reason for them and they are skeptical of hierarchy, experts, institutions, advertising, and formal religion.[41] They may not have the patience, time, or perseverance to go to a level beyond the basic and obvious and need to learn personal management. They are more results-oriented than time-oriented.

• **Communication:** Visual media is a critical form of communication to them. Andy Crouch asserts that, similar to how the shift to writing required the skills we call literacy, so the visual culture of the Millennials and Gen Xers requires its own skills—visualcy.[42] Story is a great way to lend meaning—they understand things better when told it through real life application. Due to the growth of technical communication, their oral and written skills may be seen as lacking by older generations. They may also lack critical thinking and problem solving as an individual because they have always done this in groups.

• **Systematic Thinking:** They are not systematic thinkers, tending to pick and choose what seems to make sense without the deep thinking that makes sure what they believe in one area does not contradict another. They don't ask, "How does this work?" They ask, "How can I work this?" They want to know the "why" behind things. When they ask *"Why?" they aren't necessarily being* defiant as it seem to older generations—Millennials really do want to know "why." The question is asked for understanding, not for a defense of what was done.

Quick Comparisons

Work attitudes:

Traditionalists:	The boss is always right
Baby Boomers:	Live to work
Generation X:	Work to live
Millennials:	Work my way

Values:

Traditionalists:	Tradition/loyalty
Baby Boomers:	Hard work/achieving success
Generation X:	Flexibility/life balance
Millennials:	Challenge/work that matters

Motivation:

Traditionalists:	"Good job"
Baby Boomers:	Symbols of success
Generation X:	Immediate feedback, training
Millennials:	Social justice

Information:

Traditionalists:	Little, local
Baby Boomers:	Power
Generation X:	Accessible to all
Millennials:	Needs trusted filter

Technology:

Traditionalists:	Foreigners
Baby Boomers:	Third year language students
Generation X:	Learned through immersion
Millennials:	Natives

Authority:

Traditionalists:	Respect authority
Baby Boomers:	Challenge authority
Generation X:	Don't trust authority
Millennials:	Don't appreciate rigid hierarchal authority

Dealing with Conflict:

Traditionalists:	Best avoided
Baby Boomers:	The boss is right, work through proper channels
Generation X:	Swallowed, but look for a way out of the situation
Millennials:	To be openly discussed and dealt with as a group

Assets:

Traditionalists:	Hard working
Baby Boomers:	Loyal, mature; team perspective
Generation X:	Independent, creative, adaptable
Millennials:	Technologically savvy, driven to learn

Training/Learning:

Traditionalists:	I learned it the hard way, you can too.
Baby Boomers:	Train people too much and they'll leave.
Generation X:	The more people learn, the more they stay.
Millennials:	Continuous learning is a way of life.

Maslow's Hierarchy (importance at work)
Traditionalists: Safety
Baby Boomers: Belongingness and self-esteem
Generation X: Self-esteem
Millennials: Self-esteem and self-actualization

Work:
Traditionalists: Build a legacy
Baby Boomers: Build a career
Generation X: Build a career that is portable
Millennials: Build a career that makes a difference

Family Dinner:
Traditionalists: Lucky to have it
Baby Boomers: Eat by 5
Generation X: Eat without mom and dad
Millennials: Eat out or take out

Love Connections:
Traditionalists: Letters
Baby Boomers: Telephone
Generation X: Email
Millennials: Text, Facebook, Twitter

"Jump"
Traditionalists: How high?
Baby Boomers: Why?
Generation X: Who's asking me to?
Millennials: Who is going to jump with me?

Working Together

Low performing employees are often low performing because they are misplaced or poorly managed.[43] Negative stereotypes and lack of understanding of skill sets and motivations can contribute to this. In working together, it is important to see you can take what may be common negative stereotypes about each generation and flip them to what you can appreciate about each generation.

GENERATION	NEGATIVE STEREOTYPES	ASPECTS TO APPRECIATE
Traditionalists	Boring, conservative, too compliant	Know corporate history, wise, appreciate structure and longevity, understand what is needed for financial stability
Baby Boomers	Self-centered, unscrupulous, materialistic, superficial	Understand timelines, goal orientations, results focus, strong work ethic
Gen Xers	Pessimistic, unmotivated, loner mentality	Work /life balance, entrepreneurial spirit, independence
Millennials	Entitled, impulsive, demanding, immature	Understanding of social networking and other technical solutions, creative, optimistic, great team players

In *Working Across Generations,* certain tasks are identified that each generation needs to focus on, what can frustrate each generation about the others and what each generation has to uniquely offer. The recommendations are summarized below:

TRADITIONALISTS:

Focus: Contribution (think through exit plan and leaving a legacy, leave a record of successes/ failures in both writing and in the younger leaders of the organization).

What they offer other generations: Mentor and remind (listen and offer honest assessments).

How they can discourage other generations: Dismiss them, neglect to pass on information and legacy, opt out.

BOOMERS:

Focus: Assessment (assess influence and power, use it to unite people and make needed changes to move forward, consolidate learning to pass on).

What they offer other generations: Partnering with Gen Xers for leadership. Give them power and authority. Challenge Millennials to develop leadership and give them encouragement. Help Traditionalists' legacies to be a positive encouragement to all.

How they can discourage other generations: Refuse to plan for or support new leadership while trying to stay in power.

GEN XERS:
Focus: Establishment (Move focus from self to the field, gain mastery, expand networks, find opportunities to incorporate ideas, continue learning, and broadening experiences).

What they offer other generations: Bridge between the Boomers and the Millennials, partner with Boomers and learn from Traditionalists to create ongoing growth and leadership, honor Millennial innovation and creativity.

How they can discourage other generations: Remain alienated and opt out of leadership.

MILLENNIALS:
Focus: Development (acquire skills, knowledge, analytical abilities, move quickly among tasks, extend view of work and possible roles, develop identity with communities of choice).

What they offer other generations: Be active learners of what has gone on before, be willing to voice opinions and insights in a respectful manner, allow themselves to make mistakes and learn from them.

How they can discourage other generations: Ignore previous generations and neglect to learn from the past.[44]

Misti Burmeister remarks, "Focusing on proficiencies that young professionals 'should have' wastes *time and energy* which could be more productively spent helping them gain the skills necessary to successfully carry out the organization's vision and mission. After all, isn't that the task of most importance?"[45]

YOUR TURN

Joe/Samantha

Joe has been with a non-profit organization for twenty years. He wanted to retire, but the economy changed his plans. Samantha just graduated from college with a degree in psychology. She joined the organization as an intern because she could not find a paying job following graduation. She feels she has some great ideas about how to move the organization forward with social media and group leadership, but doesn't understand why she seems to be ignored in meetings. Joe feels she is disrespectful in the way she voices her opinion, and thinks her responses are too simplistic when she doesn't understand the organization's history. Based on what you've read so far, how would you help them work together?

_____

_____

_____

Jennifer/Rebecca

Jennifer has been with her organization for eight years. She saw the CEO leave for reasons of moral failure. She is waiting to see how the organization responds, but has thought often of leaving to start her own business as a consultant. Rebecca has been with the organization for fifteen years and feels that Jennifer is unmotivated and stagnating in her position. However, Rebecca can't afford another turnover on her team. What would you tell them?

_____

_____

_____

Steve/New Hires

Steve has been with the company for almost forty years. He is what you would call a man of "quiet wisdom." He has left quite a legacy of hard work, strength, and integrity. You have observed that the new group of interns and new-hires seem to be separated from everyone else. They seem entitled and act like they are not interested in fitting into the way things are. They want change, but older employees think they have a very naïve perspective. How might you help the new hires become more engaged, utilizing Steve's unique position and skills?

_____

_____

_____

SUGGESTIONS:

Joe/Samantha

Explaining to both Joe and Samantha where Baby Boomers and Millennials have come from and what makes them tick should help them understand each other a bit better. Brainstorm with them about how to appreciate the past while leaving room for new ideas, and how to be respectful of protocol while creating venues for all voices in the organization to be heard. Have Joe tell Samantha what he has loved about working for the organization over the years, and what some of his favorite corporate accomplishments are. Have Samantha tell Joe what things she sees are working and what things might have run their course based on her fresh perspective. Have them work on finding ways to affirm each other.

Jennifer/Rebecca

Even though the concern for her turnover rate may be the motivator, Rebecca needs to sit down and have a conversation with Jennifer, letting her know she genuinely cares about Jennifer and her working situation. She can ask Jennifer what she likes about her job and what she feels she does well, with the desire to help her incorporate those skills as frequently as possible. Also, knowing the distrust many Xers have for corporate leadership, Rebecca can let Jennifer know what the company is going to do to keep what happened with the prior CEO from happening again. Set up a regular time for them to touch base in the future for ongoing progress monitoring.

Steve/New Hires

Steve would be a potentially great mentor to younger generations and new hires. His patience and lack of need to compete puts him in a perfect place to help the young hires integrate into the organization. By either mentoring the leaders of the younger group or by having a group mentoring scenario, Steve can be a listening ear for the new hires, encouraging their passion and ideas for their new position. Steve can also educate these new hires on corporate culture and how to find a path to leadership within the organization—how to voice their opinions in a way that reflects respect as well as a desire for innovation.

STATISTICS

General:
• 50% of the workforce could retire today.

• Nearly 90% of the world's top 200 firms are led by Boomers or older. Only 23 are lead by members of Generation X.[46]

• There's been an increase in adults who say there is a major generation gap—60% in 1979 up to 79% in 2009.[47]

Millennials: Because of the current "buzz" about Millennials entering the workforce and the effect it is have on organizations, a number of recent studies have found that:

• Millennials are biologically different due to growing up with technology. MRIs prove this—only 17% of our neurons are linked at birth, the rest are soft wired through experiences that last through the early 20s.[48]

• At least 75% of Millennials sleep with a cell phone within arm's reach.[49]

• Only one in five Millennials take the initiative to connect with their superiors.[50]

• The US Department of Labor reports that the average Millennial will hold ten to fourteen jobs by the time they are thirty-eight years old.[51]

• A SelectMind study found that nearly half (46%) of Millennials rate the availability of support/networking programs for employees with common interests as a very important factor, compared to only 36% for the other generations.[52]

• The *Wall Street Journal* reports that the "Millennial generation rated their managers more highly than did Generation Xers or Baby Boomers. Sixty-eight percent of surveyed Millennials rated their manager's performance 'good' or 'very good.'"[53]

• Pew Research found that Millennials are on track to being the most educated generation—40% of 18-24 year olds are enrolled in or have graduated from college. They also found that 23% of Millennials who work full time say they are "very happy" with their lives.[54]

• A study done by UCLA in 2005 revealed that 66% of their incoming freshmen believe it is essential to help others in need, which is the highest it has been in twenty-five years. They also found that 70% volunteered on a weekly basis.[55]

• A Kaiser Foundation Study found that Millennials spend 6.5 hours per day communicating through an electronic medium and are exposed to 8.3 hours of media per day (due to their multitasking abilities).[56]

We all want the same job, right?

Job promotions are another place you may misjudge attractive opportunities to recruit and promote employees because many of these practices are still influenced by the Boomer mentality of more money, higher position motivators. You may find that:

* The Generation Xer gets a promotion but is not excited because relocation is required. The Baby Boomer does not understand this—she would have relocated at any time for a promotion.

* The Millennial takes a job in a "green" company even when the pay is less.

* The Traditionalist comes back to the work force after retiring in a lower position than when she left because she desires the community and opportunities for mentoring younger employees.

Giga what?

Technology to the younger generation means fun, and they are comfortable with it. They grew up with video games, cell phones, and iPods. In contrast, the older generations use technology to get work done—it is something to be learned and used.

SECTION 3
BEST PRACTICES

GENERAL

• **Communication:** Everyone holds responsibility to communicate clearly and make sure they have been understood accurately. Everyone needs to find common reference points, a common language. Make organizational vision and mission clear so that it defies generational blinders.

• **Diverse Learning Networks:** Rob Cross, a professor at University of Virginia, describes the need for diverse learning networks. This means intentionally working on more direct connections with people in order to keep high performers. He recommends twelve to fifteen intentional relationships, with four to six of them being of the mentoring type. These relationships should go beyond direct job function, across departments, beyond staff hierarchy and even geography.[57]

> "We…need to be humble about the value of our experience. All our experience deals with the past, yet all our problems and challenges are of the future." —Leonard Sweet, Summoned to Lead

• **Mentoring:** Gen Xers and Millennials don't trust institutions, but they will commit to people they trust. Relationship precedes action, and the belief in the authenticity of a person is essential.

They are encouraged by mutually-beneficial mentoring because engagement and relationships are critical. If they see genuine belief in them, they will flourish. So older generations should encourage younger generations through authentic faith in their abilities. Let the older ones share their inspiration, come alongside the younger generations and champion them, be their advocates and their risk buffers. Get behind their desire for change and help them steer to a place worth changing for. Make sure you model the behavior you want from them—avoid negative comments and cattiness and model team work and respect instead. Institute a fair way to pass out rewards and discipline. Find their passion and tap into it. Create a compelling vision for them to put their efforts behind.

> *"We need to think of ourselves as facilitators instead of transmitters." —Kathy Koch, Celebrate Kids*

- **Distance Mentoring:** True to its name, distance mentoring is not face-to-face, but done usually through some type of electronic means. It is becoming more viable with all of the emerging electronic options available and since the younger generations are comfortable with this type of communication.

- **Group mentoring:** This practice makes it so you can mentor more people at once—something Millennials in particular crave. You can use group sharing technologies like Google Docs, Skype video conferencing, and group conference calls.

 **IN ACTION**

GO THE DISTANCE

Distance mentoring can have very practical benefits. I was able to finish my dissertation with two key advisors who were not in close physical proximity, but had the exact skills and experiences I needed. Remaining open to the possibilities that distance mentoring offered gave me access to wisdom I would not otherwise have tapped into locally.

One mentor can participate, or even more than one. The group can consist of peers, which feels natural to Millennials in particular. Group mentoring is also a cost-effective way to acclimate and train new employees.

- **Anonymous mentoring:** This happens when mentees and mentors are paired up outside their companies (the mentee's company usually foots the bill). Identities remain anonymous to protect the organization's informational capital, competitive conflict of interest, and reputations, but the generic advice from a perspective not bogged down by specific corporate biases is quite helpful.[58]

• **Vision cast:** Paint a vision of working for a higher purpose for the younger generations—one that makes sense to them and excites their passion. Passion and vision can bind all groups together. "A vision/mission should be something so empowering

119

that individuals on the team are excited to do their best every day."[59] A strong vision offering concrete steps in which to achieve it gives workers confidence in the organization and confidence in their ability to move forward.

WHY PASSION MATTERS

As we think about goals to move ourselves forward and help us grow, we are motivated to act on these goals, especially when they are based on what truly matter to us. Tapping into passion dumps gasoline on the fire of motivation. You know that feeling—that rush you experience when you are working on something you know matters, which you are good at, or that you know will make a difference. That's passion. Passion helps us press forward when things begin to stall. It helps us put value to the small steps we take in order to get to a goal we care about.

I was inspired by the head of our IT department, whose passion for helping the leaders of the organization connect in a way that would really help them share leadership best practices, training exercises, and encourage leaders in remote locations. His passion led him not only to put in long hours, but also to think creatively in ways that had not been done before. It helped him push though and advocate for his projects in a strong and unique way despite the financial crunch the organization was feeling. The result was a great interactive information sharing network that is still being used today. This sharing system actually ended up increasing the effectiveness of the remote leaders, and the benefit was felt throughout the whole organization.

• **Use social networking:** Different types of mentoring relationships and keeping up with fluctuating learning needs can be accommodated by social media. But keep in mind that you'll need to suggest trusted sources and filters to keep the information explosion in check.

• **Give feedback:** Help your people see what unique contribution they make to the goals of the organization—no superficial pats on the head. People want accurate, unbiased evaluation and documentation of work performance. Younger generations want feedback, but also the encouragement that you will work with them to find solutions to any barriers they encounter.

• **The power of story:** People of all ages enjoy a good story. Take the time to learn about the people you work with, ask them about their story—where they have been, what they have done, whom they have known. The connection will grow and you will be more tolerant of each other in challenging work situations. Even very private people can usually tell a story.

STORY OF LEADERSHIP

Everyone loves a compelling story. And when that story is true and part of the life of someone we care about, it can become a powerful encouragement. Mentoring relationships are the perfect place to share these stories. One story that helped me was of my mentor's trips to Afghanistan. As a female leader, she voluntarily humbled herself to appear submissive in order to gain entrée to the community and help Afghani women. This made me realize that there is more than one way to show strong leadership.

• **Work with diverging motivations:** People need to see each other as competent, authentic, able to create meaningful connections, accountable, and dependable. The following are three ways to help people find their voices in your organization, regardless of their generational biases:[60]

- To overcome the conflict of appreciating the past versus appreciating the new, construct a vision and passion to be a unifying call to action. Creating a learning culture, where everyone's strengths are celebrated, will foster overall appreciation for one another.

- To overcome the conflict of playing by the rules versus flexibility and wanting to "do it my way," give everyone responsibility for outcomes and results. Let them try different things and make it safe for them to make mistakes. This levels the playing field for all involved and puts the focus on where they are going rather than on how they get there.

- To overcome the conflict of paying your dues versus wanting a voice now, give everyone a way to voice his or her ideas. When people know they will be heard, they are more willing to contribute. More authentic contributions from a diverse pool of talent can only help move your organization forward.

TRADITIONALISTS

• Ask them to share their experiences.

• Verbally show respect for their experience and wisdom.

• Put them in positions where they can be social.

• Have them mentor your younger generations.

BABY BOOMERS

• Show respect for the work they have done and the experiences they have had.

• Rather than just giving your opinion without solicitation, ask Boomers if they would mind hearing your perspective.

• Help Boomers prepare for their exit, to leave well, leave a legacy, and leave for something they deem important.

GENERATION X

• In working with Xers to promote a climate of innovation in the face of constant change and ambiguity, Tamara Erikson suggests:

> Understand the Xers' importance placed on relationships and increased collaborative capacity, their inclination to question basic assumptions enhances their diversity in perspectives and thus asking compelling questions will release these perspectives, embrace complexity and welcome disruptive information.

When you try to make things too simple, you miss out on the best solutions. Sometimes the solutions are complex because the challenges are. Xers have faced challenges in their growing up environment, and are astute and seeing back up plans to keep innovation moving forward.[61]

• People need a cause to rally behind. Shaping a strong corporate identity will bring together needed synergies with all of the generations represented in an organization. This will aid in integrating work and personal values, which Xers value in particular.

• Appreciate the diversity of multiple points of view. Xers are much more comfortable with this than Boomers. Boomers grew up and have worked in a power structure that is played as a zero-sum game where in order for someone to win, someone else has to lose. This can make the Boomer less tolerant of diversity. If they are able to judge someone or something as less, they win. Xers see the world as a place where many people can win at the same time—one does not necessarily have to lose value in order for another to win. Compromise and working toward common goals enable the simultaneous success of multiple people.

• Gen X employees are particularly jaded by corporate corruption and feelings of being unappreciated. Help them trust your organization by communicating the value your organization places on them. Building strong mentoring relationships can support this process effectively.

MILLENNIALS

• **Feedback:** Millennials crave immediate feedback, and often. Susan Hutt at Workbrain/Infor Consulting instituted an online, on-demand assessment system that limits feeds back to 140 characters—great for those used to Twitter and texting. They don't see it as curt, just quick and immediate. What a great way to review Millennials more frequently! You can't teach them only through rules and structure—the relational aspect is needed as well. Mentoring is also a great way to give feedback and teach them what they need to know. They want mentors, but have a difficult time finding them. They want a road map for success, to don't know how to get there. They are used to being told what to do from parents, with lots of advice of how to be successful. Through strong mentoring relationships, help them find trusted sources of information, find what is useful and truthful, help them learn to categorize, and then help them make decisions based on what they have learned.

• **Creativity:** Encourage their natural creativity and curiosity. Teach them to ask: Is there a better way? Help them put what they know together in a systematic way, and challenge them when things don't fit to figure it out themselves (don't give them the answers). Help them find their own way. Set aside blocks of time for creativity and focused problem solving. Millennials are used to co-creation—work with them with this in mind. Make it their success. Shift away from positional bargaining to joint problem solving.

• **Information:** They have grown up assuming there are choices for everything, from what and where to eat, to where to work and live. They have had access to all kinds of information for years—more than they know what to do with. They think globally in a way unprecedented in earlier generations. They need trusted filters and help to process the information, putting value to it, and prioritizing it. Mentors can help them use information in a meaningful way. Provide information that is portable, transferrable, paperless, and accessible all the time.

• **Structure:** Millennials will share what they know—they do it regularly. Help them find what is worthy of their time and energy to share. Set up rewards and incentives for completing certain benchmarks or learning and development exercises. Help them see the path that will lead to their success and the specific steps they need to take to get there. Help them see that they have a responsibility for the results.

• **Cross-train:** Cross-train Millennials for jobs throughout the organization. Let them try out a number of positions before you finally place them. They will learn the company better, may have new perspectives to offer, and can use their penchant for creativity and innovation with a more well-rounded view of the overall company.

• **Reverse mentoring:** Allow Millennials to become mentors to older generations. Millennials' comfort and expertise with social media and electronic modes of finding information can be beneficial to older generations. Reverse mentoring should also increase positive exposure for the younger workers, along with expanding their education in other areas of the company.

KEY POINTS/HIGHLIGHTS

- There are four generations in the current workforce: Traditionalists, Baby Boomers, Gen Xers, and Millennials.

- Each generation comes from very different backgrounds and sets of experiences, which have shaped their perceptions and consequently their outward actions.

- When you can learn about each generation and understand how and why people think and act the way they do, you can move from irritation to appreciation and respect, from complaining to championing.

- Appreciating each other leads to greater productivity.

- It is critical to empower and encourage each generation to contribute what only they can.

- Key strategies include:

  -Equip people to find flexibility with accountability.
  -Help each individual find a path for their individual contributions and place for leadership.
  -Support clear open and authentic communication.
  -Encourage passion and vision as a connecting point.
  -Promote a learning culture and a value on curiosity of judgment.

SO WHAT

WHY THIS WILL MAKE A DIFFERENCE IN YOUR ORGANIZATION

The clash between generations is causing issues in the workplace that are leading to lower productivity, frustrated and disconnected employees, and stagnant organizations. With an increase in respect, understanding, and appreciation of the distinctions of each generation, organizations can move forward and, in many situations, garner a competitive edge. Reducing conflict, frustration, and misunderstandings can pave the way for increased productivity and open doors to new ideas, moving employees from an hourly focus to an outcome focus.

Mentoring promotes healthy relationships and a learning atmosphere, empowering employees to work together to produce the unique synergies that only very unique and different people working together can produce.

TAKING IT FORWARD

Take time to write down any reflections, points to remember, or next steps that you will take forward as a result of what you have considered while reading this chapter.

_____

_____

_____

_____

_____

_____

_____

_____

_____

_____

_____

_____

SECTION 3
EXERCISES

1. PRACTICE AWARENESS: Listen to yourself and your colleagues and see what comparisons are made between different generations and how things are done. You will be surprised at how often this happens. Make a conscious effort to reduce this, or talk about these differences in a positive light instead of with irritation.

2. POWER: Discuss the way power is viewed by your organization—its importance, how it manifests itself, how it is changing, how it should change. Note differences in perspective on this held by each generation. Discuss how to work together more respectfully with this in mind.

3. FOCUSED GENERATIONAL DISCUSSION:

•Divide into single generational groups.

Part one: Using the generational descriptions earlier in the section, discuss accomplishments, challenges, and what would be helpful for the other generations to understand. How has your generation affected your view of work?

Part two: Discuss your perceptions of the other three generations. What do they respect? What frustrates them?

Part three: Discuss within your group leadership styles that you see. What are the differences? What works? What's frustrating?

Part four: Reconvene with all generational groups together. Share the discussion points and perceptions each group came to. Do these perceptions ring true with the other generational groups? Why or why not? How can these differing attributes be used to better the organization? Discuss how knowing this can help you work together with less judgment and more respect.

• With a generationally diverse group, have a worker from one generation describe an experience they had with someone from another generation. Then have the person from the described generation explain why things went the way they did. Discuss how this might affect their perceptions in the future.

• Brainstorm current work challenges. Break into smaller units to brainstorm solutions. See what differences there are between the generational groups. Facilitate a discussion about it.

4. MOTIVATORS: (adapted from an exercise by Lorraine Bosse-Smith[62]) Rate from 1 to 10 the attributes on the left—1 being what that generation values most and 10 being what they value least. Compare to the answer key that follows.

	TRADITIONAL	BOOMER	GEN X	MILLENNIAL
Competition				
Flexibility/Life Balance				
High levels of interaction				
Immediate				
Feedback				
Symbols of success				
Loyalty/ Tradition				
Enjoyment of work				
Ability to make decisions/ autonomy				
Group/team participation				

Here are suggested rankings: Compare your answers.

	TRADITIONAL	BOOMER	GEN X	MILLENNIAL
Competition	5	2	7	7
Flexibility/Life Balance	4	8	1	5
Organizations that are socially responsible	7	5	5	1
Immediate Feedback	9	7	2	3
Symbols of success	2	1	9	8
Loyalty/ Tradition	1	6	8	9
Enjoyment of work	3	4	4	4
Ability to make decisions/ autonomy	8	3	3	6
Group/team participation	6	9	6	2

Do you agree with this ranking? Why or why not?

_____

_____

_____

_____

_____

_____

_____

Notice how very different some of the lines are as you move across the generations. How can you account for this in your work environment so that you increase job satisfaction and keep productivity high?

_____

_____

_____

_____

_____

_____

_____

_____

5. PREPARE FOR LEADERSHIP TRANSITIONS: What will be different once the current leaders transition, what did they accomplish, what did they bring to the organization that will be lost? Celebrate what they contributed and the legacy that they leave. What holes will they leave behind? How can they be proactively filled? What has worked well in previous transitions? What should be avoided?

6. APPRECIATION: Make it a regular habit to have your employees show appreciation for each other. When you look for things to appreciate, it overshadows irritations you might feel because your focus is on the positive. Regular appreciation is also encouraging and motivating to people in your organization.

• Give packets of 25 stars to each member of your team to distribute among those who have encouraged them.

• Set up an encouragement twitter for people to give quick pats on the back electronically.

• Distribute paper and Post-It notes. Have each person put their name on a sheet of the paper. Ask everyone write something they appreciate about each person on a Post-It and stick it to the paper with the corresponding name on it.

SECTION 4

MENTORING THROUGH GLOBAL DIVERSITY

THEY DID WHAT?

The groans were audible. The college students in my Ideas and Issues class were not overly excited about their latest assignment. I had asked them to have a conversation with someone from a different culture.

"What if they won't talk to us?" asked one frustrated student.

"What if I don't know someone from another culture?" asked another.

Uh oh, I thought, *this was the response I had been afraid of.* I was trying to teach the idea of listening for "touchpoints"—something in common between you and a person from a different culture. I naively thought the idea would excite the class as much as it had me, but I was wrong.

"That's the beauty of the assignment. You don't have to do any fancy speeches or try to convince them about anything. All I am asking you to do is create a safe place to connect with you by listening to them."

"So we're supposed to just *listen* to them? What if they start cutting down our way of doing things? What do we do then?"

"You just might find that listening lowers the need to be combative like that," I replied, hoping to lessen the anxiety in the room. "As you listen, try to hear touch points—things you have in common with the other person. You might be surprised with what you find out."

They left the classroom, a cloud of gloom almost visible over their heads.

Yet the exercise had surprising results. By the next class, the students were buzzing with the news of how they had been able to connect with people from other cultures. They realized that, though these people *seemed* so different, they had a lot in common, such as love for their families, the desire to do a good job, and the need for friendship. They realized that cultural differences don't have to keep them disconnected.

The electronic world has given us access to every corner of the globe. What was once global is becoming local, a phenomenon sometimes referred to as "glocal." In our homes and offices, cultures have been thrust against one another. People from other cultures are more available, helping organizations to tap into this diverse learning environment. Unfortunately, people assume too often that, because they have some things in common, people are basically like us and will communicate, expect, perceive, and respond to life and work challenges the same way they do. Even though it would seem that the familiarity that globalization breeds would decrease cultural differences, research shows that this is not the case. Globalization actually *increases* these differences. In addition, the diversity highlighted by globalization is making things more difficult for organizations that work across nations. One study found that 50% of overseas mergers and acquisitions produce negative returns to shareholders due to cultural clashes.[63]

> *"Prejudice is never easy unless it can pass itself off as reason." —William Hazlitt.*

So what can be done? Enter cross-cultural mentoring as a strategy to maximize "glocalization." Mentoring is a proven strategy for organizations working through many challenges of diversity because it creates bonds and relationships that transcend differences. It promotes *appreciation* instead of *irritation* and *synergy* instead of *division*. For harmony within diversity, mentoring is a must.

SO WHAT EXACTLY IS CULTURE AND CULTURAL MENTORING?

Culture: A shared system of beliefs, attitudes, and values that create expectation and norms for behaviors.

Cross-cultural Mentoring: Appreciating cultural differences while developing a trust relationship that facilitates culturally-appropriate steps toward growth.

As much as people would like to be immune to the discomfort of the unknown, they often approach others from a fear of the unfamiliar rather than curiosity for something new. This is different than the diversity they experience through generational and gender differences—with these, they often assume they know how the other person feels. They aren't as "foreign" to them as global differences which they may approach differently, admitting their lack of knowledge and understanding. Because of this, you may avoid mentoring relationships with people of other cultures because they seem too difficult, too "foreign," too hard to build a trusting, close relationship.

With the global expansion of business, forming these relationships is becoming less of an option and more of a mandate. But it doesn't have to be something you do out of desperation or force—cross-cultural mentoring can be a great opportunity for the growth spurred by diverse perspectives. Think of all that can be learned from someone who has grown up in a different environment: politically, socio-economically, ethnically, educationally...the possibilities for learning are truly endless.

How do you take the first step toward cross-cultural mentoring relationships? First, become aware of some of the cultural differences you might encounter.

What differences have you observed when working with people from a different culture?

_____

_____

_____

_____

_____

_____

How did they deal with information distribution?

_____

_____

With negotiations/conflict?

_____

_____

With social events/ friendships?

_____

_____

With leadership?

_____

_____

These are just a few areas in which you may have noticed behavior different than your own.

Lois Zachary talks about cross-cultural differences, noting that people can make a big mistake when they assume their way of thinking is identical, or even similar, to the values, protocol, time and punctuality, spatial distance, authority figures (including mentors), decision-making, and appropriate humor of other cultures.[64]

The culture you are born into and where you are raised actually wires your brain to work a certain way. This is why people from different cultures can be so completely different from each other. One thing we all have in common is that people are all born egocentric and ethnocentric. It is only when you intentionally address this in your thinking that you will be able to form different perspectives from those shaped in you as you grew up.

> *"Nature never rhymes her children nor makes two men alike." —Ralph Waldo Emerson*

INTERNATIONAL ASSIGNMENTS

One of the most dramatic places people experience cultural differences is when they accept international assignments. Below are the current reasons for the assignments and the ways that organizations are preparing people for these transitions.

International assignments are currently made most often to fill an immediate skill need (at a rate of 66.7%, indicating a high/very high extent as to why these assignments are made), for leadership development (40.2%), to develop a more global corporate culture (37.0%), and employee development (30.1%).[65]

Preparation for employee success is most often accomplished by a preview trip to the host country (36.6% of the time), preview trip with spouse (30.5%), personal assessments of suitability (25.4%), language training (23.9%), cultural training prior to assignment (23.9%), and cultural training in host country (17.8%).[66]

THE DIFFERENCE A HIGH CQ MAKES

A Cultural Intelligence Quotient is a common assessment in cross cultural exploration. Developing this helps with cross cultural communication and relationship building. It is defined by David Livermore as the ability to effectively reach across the chasm of cultural difference in ways that are loving and respectful. He divides the CQ into four categories:

• **Knowledge CQ:** The breadth of understanding cross-cultural issues and differences.

• **Interpretive CQ:** The degree to which you're mindful and aware when you interact cross-culturally.

• **Perseverance CQ:** Your level of interest, drive, and motivation to adapt cross-culturally.

• **Behavioral CQ:** The extent to which you appropriately change your verbal and nonverbal actions when you interact cross-culturally.[67]

Although American culture frowns upon profiling people based on their ethnic background, it is helpful to research the norms and mores of other cultures. It's when you use that information to form hard and fast judgments that you've crossed the line. Or when you decide that something about a culture is wrong and then try to change it. Or if you flat out tell someone from another culture that his/her view on a certain issue is wrong.

 IN ACTION

CROSSED WIRES

Dr. Les Hirst, a colleague of mine who has worked cross-culturally for years, tells the story of a professor who, in his desire to be humble and approachable, insisted that his students call him by his first name. This was so uncomfortable and upsetting for the Asian students in his class that it greatly hindered their learning. When someone finally pointed this out to the professor, he of course allowed them to use a more formal address when speaking to him. Clearly this professor did not have harmful motivations in trying to be more amicable—he just wasn't thinking of the cross-cultural effects his behavior would have. Raising our cultural CQ may help us become more effective in our relationships with others.

David Thomas notes that two people of different cultures are likely to treat their relationship as more fragile than other relationships they may have–he calls it "protective hesitation." They may not be as willing to be open about sensitive issues and they may be more afraid of confrontation because they don't want to offend or be thought of as anti-____ *(fill in the blank)*. The result is that these relationships may have difficulty forming, developing, and maturing.[68]

You may become unsure about whether authentically strong relationships can be formed, and may be concerned that the potential difficulty in truly identifying with someone so different is too high. It may be unclear how role-modeling should look, what aspects of our culture you should hold tight and what you should hold in an open hand to better facilitate connection with others. You may wonder how to be authentic without making the other person uncomfortable. You may even be overly concerned about what others might think and allow that to unduly influence your behavior.

In the face of all these fears, mentoring can be a great tool for helping your employees work in cross-cultural environments. Researcher David Thomas stresses that the people who adjust the best when they are the ethnic minority at work all have a network of relationships where others are focused on helping them develop and grow, which includes mentors from their own and other cultures. [69] Naomi S. Brown's doctoral study of Asian professional women also shows the benefit of finding mentors from the dominant (in this case, Caucasian) culture.[70] Building relationships through mentoring can lay the groundwork for significant cross-cultural learning.

In this section, we take a look at some of the differing perspectives you may run across. The goal is to help you see that other perspectives are not necessarily right or wrong, but are simply different. You don't just want to add to the differences, you need to use them and regularly encourage each other to bring all of who you are to all you do, no matter where you're from.

> *"It is well to remember that the entire population of the universe, with one trifling exception, is composed of others." —John Andrew Holmes*

Trust

A high CQ is important to building trust across cultural lines. Knowing about other cultures, being aware of how you interact, being motivated to learn and show respect, and acting appropriately can all be trust builders. "Trust lowers the cost of doing business" says Deepika Bajaj, Founder of Invincibelles.[71] It unleashes energy and confidence, shares power and promotes the trying of new things. Trust even has the practical effect of not having to double-check work. Just think of the time and money saved if lawyers never needed to be involved. Bottom line, trust means doing what you say you will do and behaving with integrity.

Trust, however, is developed differently in different cultures. For example, looking people in the eye may be important in western culture, but may be disrespectful in Asian cultures. In Africa and Latin America, inviting others into your home and you going to theirs is critical to building trust. In Latin America, parents are important mentors to their kids, from birth into adulthood. It is important to show respect and deference to parents and value the mentoring they have provided before you can build a trusting mentoring relationship with the potential mentee.

But do you know what the one universal element that builds trust is? **Listening**. Attentively and actively. Listening with focus, without distraction. Allowing for interruptions can be a trust buster in many cultures.

In some cultures, requiring direct **accountability** can be a trust-buster—the perception is that by holding them accountable, they think you don't trust them to do what was asked. In Asian cultures, it is important to avoid direct confrontation where a person could lose face. But, in the Western culture, holding people accountable in a respectful way can actually build trust.

A **mentoring** trust builder in most cultures is being willing to attend outside activities. Many people from community-based cultures place high value on their on an integration of mentoring and their full social community. This means inviting your mentee or mentor into your community outside your work environment, and attending theirs if asked. If you can't open your life to your mentee or mentor, and if you are unwilling to enter their world outside of the workplace, then it would be better to not begin a mentoring relationship with someone from a community-based culture. The disconnect will be felt with your mentee or mentor, and may even be detrimental.

A quick caution related to building trust-based mentoring relationships: Many cultures don't understand the idea that a mentoring relationship, once begun, should stop at some point. While the relationship may become a much less formal arrangement, you simply cannot fall off the face of the earth, or it will be worse than if you had not mentored at all. Your mentees may think they did something to cause the break in the relationship and this can be hurtful to any growth they have experienced.

THE WEST VS. THE TWO-THIRDS WORLD

There can be quite a difference between Western and two-thirds world cultures. Western cultures tend to view life as categorical, black-and-white, a timeline with discreet events. By contrast, Duane Elmer paints this contrasting picture of the Two-Thirds World culture: "[They] tend to be more holistic in their view of life. They see life not so much as a timeline but as a tapestry where one sees threads and colors touching, overlapping and re-inforcing each other, forming a whole that has its own beauty and integrity."[72] People from success-driven Western cultures consider self-esteem something that is universally desired, but this is not actually the case. Self-esteem really is more about group-esteem in the Two-Thirds World.[73]

> *"For you Americans, a problem is something to solve. In India, a problem is something to live around." —Quote cited by Stan Nussbaum*

Guilt-based cultures are individualistic and Western. Guilt is about the individual and what he or she has done. Shame-based cultures are common in the communal Two-Thirds World—loss of face is something that affects not just an individual; it signifi-cantly affects the community. Finding fault with an individual is common in individualistic cultures, but it is devastating in a shame-based culture.

WORDS TO FAIL BY

When The United States automaker, Chevrolet, created the "Nova" model, they were thinking in terms of astronomy—a nova is a powerful celestial event. Unfortunately, when they tried to sell the car in nearby Mexico, the sales plummeted. The car company had not realized that in Spanish "no va" means "does not go."

AMERICAN MYOPIA

While preparing for a mentoring conference in Belfast, Ireland, the leader of the effort, Sharon, sent out the program for final approval from the workshop leaders. The copy read "Shaping people who **could** shape the world" (emphasis added). I, being the gung-ho American, said, "No, this verbiage is much too passive. Wouldn't 'Shaping leaders who **will** shape the world' be better?" Sharon gently wrote back that Irish people would perceive that as too pushy and the wording would actually become a deterrent.

Respect for community comes first in many cultures. In everything they consider doing, every decision made, the effect it will have on the community as a whole, either long-term or short-term, must be considered. This flies in the face of a more Western culture that values individualism. Attitudes about the accumulation of wealth illustrate this point—Western culture lauds the growth of personal wealth as a sign of individual success and worth. The communal cultures, however, believe that to accumulate money individually is completely antisocial. Their focus is on how to share wealth to strengthen relationships, and they expect others to do the same. Personal initiative is also a place of cultural division—Western cultures prize it, while communal cultures can be insulted by it.

Respect for the elderly can also be quite different in communal cultures. Elders are part of the fabric of the community's experience and are respected for their ongoing contribution. American culture prizes youth and tends to dismiss the value of the elderly, putting them away in retirement communities.

In her book *Foreign to Familiar*, Sarah Lanier seeks to aid the reader in cross-cultural communication and relationships by highlighting the differences between hot- and cold-climate cultures. While these concepts are unfamiliar to most readers, Lanier (who is American but has lived in the Middle East, South America, Africa, Europe, and New Zealand) believes "the population of the entire world can roughly be divided into two parts. The two groups represented are 'hot-climate' (relationship-based) cultures and 'cold-climate' (task-oriented) cultures."[74] She recognizes there may be some overlap in the two categories and that personalities differ within each culture, but her findings are as follows: People in the hot-climates tend to emphasize relationships, while those in cold-climates focus on the efficient performance of tasks. She also contrasts the individualism of the cold-climates against the group-identity of the hot-climates. Privacy, highly valued in the cold, is contrasted with the inclusion found in the hot-climates. Hot-climates demonstrate much more warm hospitality, while the cold-climates are extremely conscious of time and planning. In some places, it is offensive to arrive to dinner on time because it makes it seem like you are only arriving for the task and not the relationship. In other places, it is offensive to arrive to dinner late because it seems like you are not respecting the other person's time. In a hot-climate culture, communication takes place indirectly, seeking to maintain the atmosphere of friendship, whatever the cost. In a cold climate, communication is open and direct, sometimes to the detriment of the relationship.

What's in a word?

English is the only language where the first-person pronoun "I" is capitalized while none of the other pronouns are. Other languages use the lower-case for all their pronouns. Americans only have one form of the word for "you"—most other cultures have two or three to indicate the closeness of the relationship. To find out where you stand with someone of another culture, ask which form of the word "you" they would use. The word "friend" also has a much deeper meaning than it does for Americans—the fact that you can be friends with a thousand people on Facebook would make no sense in other cultures.[75]

MOVING FROM BLACK-AND-WHITE TO CONTINUUMS

As you can see, it would be ridiculous for anyone from one culture to say that another culture's nuances of behavior are "right" or "wrong." Moving away from such black-and-white categorization toward perceiving differences as culturally-based preferences and inclinations is a critical strategy for working with people who are not like us. The framework of culturally-based choices and tendencies was developed by Dr. Geert Hofstede, who based his pioneering study on IBM affiliates in fifty countries and three regions.[76] Five dimensions of national culture were determined through his research and he placed each country and region on a continuum representing each dimension. In this way, he quantified important characteristics within each culture. Since 2001, when he proposed these continuums, scores have been developed for seventy-four countries and regions.

It is essential to remember that these are societal norms that represent the peak of a bell curve, or the "normal distribution," for that country. The country norms are not predictive of any one individual—a person may be consistent with or quite different than their country's norms based on factors like personality, gender, and generation. The norms are appropriately used to compare typical differences at the national level. They may also be used to identify differences between individuals or members of a team as a basis for understanding varied perspectives, values, and behaviors in order to boost productivity.

> *"It's strange, but wherever I take my eyes, they always see things from my point of view."*
> *—Ashleigh Brilliant*

HOFSTEDE'S CONTINUUMS

Individualism: Action is taken for

The benefit ⟷ The benefit
of the individual   of the community

Power distance: The degree to which inequality or distance in a hierarchy is accepted

Accepted ⟷ Rejected

Certainty: The degree to which people prefer rules and controls

Prefer rules, ⟷ Comfort with ambiguity,
structure   unpredictability

Achievement: Amount of focus you place on . . .

Goal achievement ⟷ Quality of life,
and work   caring for others

Time orientation:

Focus on ⟷ Guidance from the
desirable future   past/focus on present

155

Hofstede's continuum are thought-provoking. As I looked through cross-cultural research, I found a number of additional continuums that may be helpful in painting a more complete picture of cultural diversity:

View of time management:
Punctual, exact ◄────────────► Fluid

Communication styles:
Explicit ◄────────────► Implied

View of and behavior during conflict:
Direct, confrontational ◄────────► Indirect, passive

View of mentoring relationships:
Coming alongside ◄────────► Hierarchical

View of success in a mentoring relationship:
Tasks completed ◄────────► Relational strength

View of personal power:
Personal control ◄────────► Fatalistic

View of personal space:
Close ◄────────────► Distant

Status:
Achieved/worked for ◄────────► Ascribed/tradition/role

Looking at these continuums, make a mark where you personally fit. Have any of these issues caused challenges in your previous relationships?

_____

_____

_____

How could you use and appreciate cultural differences for the advantage of both parties?

_____

_____

_____

Views on things like pace of business, how much personal information you share, responsibility, choice, how to address others, dress, and gender roles can also disrupt the relationship if they are not handled with respect and discussed with genuine curiosity and care.

Country Statistics/Research

Just over 20% of the world's population is Chinese, 17% are Indian, while American and Western Europe together make up just under 10% of the world's population. With Japan adding another 1%, 11% of the world's population owns nearly 90% of the world's wealth and consumes over 50% of its products. The fifteen richest countries have a per capita income of over $11,000 per year while the fifteen poorest settle for $190.[77]

The United States has always been diverse, but is becoming increasingly so as cultures are combined through marriage. One in three Americans has someone of another race in their family, and 14.6% of newlyweds married someone of another ethnicity in 2008.[78]

YOUR TURN

Juan/Kurt

Juan's Costa Rican-based organization just opened an office in Germany. In order to make the new lines of production run smoothly with the existing ones, the organization put Juan in charge of Kurt and his Germany-based product line. Juan recognizes that, due to his leadership responsibilities, he must look at the overall processes of the organization, making sure that they run in sync with each other. But he has felt that from the beginning Kurt has been abrupt, impatient, and too focused on his German product, rather than on the company's goals.

Kurt has been running his product line for six years and has done so efficiently. He is frustrated that the new parent organization has now put his line under a bigger and seemingly amorphous production system. He thinks Juan spends too much time talking about future strategy and teamwork instead of concrete goals.

How would you encourage these men to come to a smoother working relationship? Suggestions on the following page.

_____

_____

_____

_____

_____

SUGGESTIONS

Juan/Kurt

Again, education and developing respect is critical here. Explain the benefits of both a task-orientation and a relationship-orientation and the concrete ways in which they play out in business practice. Have them discuss with each other the things that they appreciated about their companies before they came together and what they want to see preserved. Give Juan information on Kurt's performance so that he may affirm what has been going well. Give Kurt information on the parent company and why it has been successful. Encourage them to take time to talk about personal goals so that they might find points of connection. Help them brainstorm ways that would let them both know they are successful in their new positioning.

SECTION 4
BEST PRACTICES

Shades of Gray

In his book, *Cross Cultural Connections*, Duane Elmer discusses how people naturally put things into three categories: right, wrong, or different. How you categorize is informed by your upbringing, current culture, and personality.[79] A person who is less rigid and more accepting of differences will typically have a larger gray section in the bars below.[80]

Typically older generations and low multicultural exposure/experiences

Right	Differences	Wrong

Typically middle generations and average multicultural exposure/experiences

Right	Differences	Wrong

Typically younger generations and those who have been exposed to many multi-cultural experiences

Right	Differences	Wrong

It's easy to judge cultural issues as wrong because then you can dismiss them and not have to spend energy trying to understand them. But, when you suspend judgment, your interactions can be more open. It allows you to take a learning stance, valuing differences as interesting rather than right or wrong.

What judgments are you willing to suspend in order to allow other people to truly be themselves around you? Think of the last time you were in a disagreement with someone. Take a minute to fill in the box below. Write the things you disagreed with in the "right," "wrong," or "differences" categories. How do you think the other person would rate the same items? Are there ways to get the "right" and "wrong" parts moved into the "differences" category?

What did you perceive at that time?

Right	Differences	Wrong

What you think the other person perceived at the time:

Right	Differences	Wrong

After reflecting on the incident, are there items in the above two continuums that you think could be moved to the "Differences" section rather than the "wrong" section? What would those be?

_____

_____

_____

How might you approach this person differently to avoid conflict, and instead move to more of a stance of mutual appreciation?

_____

_____

_____

Monitor negative feelings. What is causing them? Is the current issue really the problem or is it past interactions that are influencing your current perception of the other person's behavior and motives? Are you able to have a different inner dialogue, one where you assume best intentions? For example, when you approach someone with whom you have had a strong disagreement in the past, can you tell yourself to relax and listen with a clean slate in your head? Can you coach yourself to let the past go so that you may be open to hearing ideas without a negative bias? If you can, you will open yourself to another source of information and another set of perceptions that may in the end be helpful.

> *"There is no such thing as an insignificant human being. To treat people that way is a kind of sin and there is no reason for it. None."*
> *—Debbie Fields*

Curious George Was Right

Sensitize yourself and call upon extra patience and a willingness to work with complexity (it would be simpler if everyone was the same, right?) Show genuine interest in each other as individuals, not just as cultures. Start questioning whether everything you do is the only or even best way. Ask questions that show sincere interest and respect. Don't assume you know what the other person is thinking or feeling. Ask questions like, "What does this mean to you?" and "How important is this to you?" Develop a genuine sense of curiosity for them and their culture. Study culture but don't generalize too much—just use it to inform your overall understanding. Look at political systems, educational systems, and history to gain a broader view of how a culture has developed.

Develop your curiosity muscles by asking, "I wonder..."—"I wonder what they think of____, I wonder how they saw this growing up? I wonder…." Practice disciplined observation—"Hmm—why did they do that? That was not the action or reaction I expected." Ask someone else from their culture to shed light on what you have observed.

CURIOSITY MADE THE CAT BETTER

My aunt has been to every continent but one, and in most cases she has stayed with the local people, eaten their food, and participated in their customs. Her experiences fill her eyes with delight as she relays the unique, exciting, and sometimes challenging stories of being a part of these different cultures. She is always positive about these experiences and the people she meets. As I thought about her "success" at living in so many places, I realized one of her greatest traits is genuine curiosity. Even while I was growing up, she would ask me questions and take on a stance of curiosity that exuded a deep care for me. It made me want to share. It made her one of my favorite people. Since then, I have seen her take the same stance with others. They love to bask in her genuine interest in them as people and in their stories. How simple to take on this stance of genuine, caring curiosity. How great an impact she has had on so many!

Find Touchpoints

Have a conversation with someone who is very different than you. Be disciplined in what you do.

• Listen, Listen, Listen. Ask a clarifying question. Listen.

• Find touchpoints in what you hear them say, things you have in common and can agree on:

- A specific topic (e.g. growth of the Internet, parenthood)

- An emotion (e.g. anger, frustration, exhaustion, love, compassion, mercy, joy, patience, humility, optimism, wisdom—which are all universally compelling)

- Specific people (e.g. spouses, coworkers, Mother Teresa)

- Past experiences (e.g. losses, successes, challenges)

   You may not agree with everything they say about a topic, but you can find points that you can appreciate: You may not agree with his highly competitive view of business, but you can agree on the common desire for success. You may not agree on his view of gun control, but you can agree on the need to feel safe. You may not agree with the way she disciplines her children, but you can agree that you both love your children enough to care that they grow up well.

• Practice appreciation. Search for bright spots. What is admirable? Fear takes significantly more energy than acceptance and appreciation does.

 **IN ACTION**

TOUCHPOINTS

While on a humanitarian aid trip to rural India, where we worked with sixty children orphaned by the tsunami, I was embarrassed at their "hero worship" of me and the four other American women I was with—worship based solely on the lighter color of our skin. Without getting into the intricacies of the caste system, suffice it to say that being valued for something so superficial was frustrating. Things leveled out, however, on our most intense day of art therapy. We had asked the children to draw something about their lives that made them sad. Most drew hauntingly descriptive pictures of the tsunami's devastation. As they shared their pictures with the group, we all, children and counselors alike, began to cry. Heart cleansing, deep tears. Clearly poignant through the differences in skin color, language, and experiences, we were all connected with the very real human emotions surrounding loss and new hope. It was a powerful reminder about how very similar we are on the things that really matter when we can look past superficial differences.

That's Not What That Means!?

Watch your idioms. It's surprising how often we use them and don't realize it. "To each his own," "the sky's the limit," "better safe than sorry," "kill two birds with one stone," "looking out for number one," all these phrases reflect the American values of individual control, power, and value of success. When these values are not held by people with whom you communicate, your meaning may be lost, misconstrued, or even cause a negative perception that you hadn't intended.

Mentoring Through It

Openness is the ability to make people feel you are safe, approachable, and receptive. They feel valued, that you accept and trust them enough to share your life with them. Acceptance then means communicating "value, regard, worth, and respect to others." Trust is the outworking of openness and acceptance. In many ways, trust makes all the difference in lasting, powerful relationships. Before you begin your mentoring relationship, go to others in that culture and ask how they would suggest you build trust with your mentee or mentor.

At the beginning of your relationship with a mentee, explore what expectations exist based on your cultural backgrounds. Cultivate intentional awareness and understanding between you both. Through active listening, be aware of your own cultural biases and then listen to the mentee to see what cultural biases he/she might have. Talk openly about biases and how they can bring depth to your relationship through varied perspectives. Don't judge negatively by history they didn't control—instead, embrace the things you have in common without making assumptions. Find places where you agree and cultivate a relationship that doesn't threaten the cultural identity of either of you.

Help people see how growth can blossom in their lives. Encourage change that is integrated and works in all their spheres of influence, whether at work, home, or play. Create a safe place to learn by promoting an environment of acceptance and respect. Promote this personal growth and better job performance by casting a powerful vision for their lives.

Don't be afraid to raise tough issues and areas where you need more understanding. Raising tough issues will actually help your relationship grow, but ignoring these issues will stunt your relationship. Set expectations and boundaries, remembering that what may be comfortable for them may not be for you. Keep in mind that the continuums above can vary within a culture as well as between cultures.

A good book series that offers practical help on cultures is *Culture Shock: China, or Culture Shock: (name of country).* This series gives a great picture of the cultures they cover and how to live well with those people. Stay away from travel books—they may be interesting but they are not really helpful in working with cross-cultural relationships.

KEY POINTS/HIGHLIGHTS

- The world is expanding—available information is increasing, as is our awareness of global differences.

- Be cautious of two assumptions:
  - Assuming we are all too alike
  - Assuming we are all too different

- Understand the Cultural Intelligence Quotient (CQ) and promote this in working in diverse situations.

- Understand where you stand on what is "right," "wrong," and just "different." See differences in terms of continuums.

- Build trust among diverse people through acceptance and respect, encouraging mentoring relationships and a learning culture.

SO WHAT

WHY THIS WILL MAKE A DIFFERENCE IN YOUR ORGANIZATION

Global reach and exposure to diverse cultures will expand your opportunity to make a mark, to make a difference. To work with these differences effectively, take the time to find touchpoints—the things you have in common—and use them for connection. Through this connection, you will find it safer to discover synergies with others that you could not imagine alone. See differences in terms of continuums, which will promote understanding and respect and foster development and creativity. Increase your learning through diverse perspectives and make space for opportunities to innovate.

Mentoring in culturally-diverse situations encourages synergy over division. Cultural Intelligence and an appreciation for diversity can be developed through mentoring relationships. Through mentoring, trust can be built and a safe place for learning and growth established so that organizations can move forward instead of being mired in unproductive misunderstandings and cultural clashes. Cross-cultural mentoring is an unmatched opportunity for the creation of new insights, opportunities, and world-changing innovation.

TAKING IT FORWARD

Take time to write down any reflections, points to remember, or next steps that you will take forward as a result of what you have considered while reading this chapter.

_____

_____

_____

_____

_____

_____

_____

_____

_____

"A wise man will make more opportunities than he finds." —Francis Bacon

SECTION 4
EXERCISES

1. DECISIONS, DECISIONS: Think about recent decisions made by your company: how do they reflect the continuums in this chapter? For each decision, consider whether you agree with it. Why or why not? Is it still a viable decision? Can you still get behind it based on appreciating cultural "differences" instead of "right" and "wrong"?

Decision: _____

Continuums: _____

_____

Agree? Why? _____

_____

Differences, right, or wrong? _____

_____

Decision: _____

Continuums: _____

_____

Agree? Why? _____

_____

Differences, right, or wrong? _____

_____

2. LEADERSHIP STYLES: What kind of leader are you? Which environments do you thrive in? Which challenge you? How is this different from leaders you have seen from another culture? What can you learn from this?

Type: _____

Environments: _____

Cultural differences: _____

Learning: _____

3. CULTURAL INTELLIGENCE QUOTIENT: Look at the following cultures. Under "Knowledge CQ," list what you think you know about each country. Under "Interpretive CQ," write what you would do to create a positive business interaction with each of these cultures. Under "Perseverance CQ," reflect on which countries you may be more comfortable/motivated to interact with and why. Under "Behavioral CQ," write what specific actions will go over well and what would cause issues in each country. Finally, discuss with your mentor/mentee any areas of cultural discomfort you might have and possible solutions to working through this discomfort.

Knowledge CQ (Understanding cross-cultural issues and differences)
- China
- Chili
- India
- Ireland
- Japan
- Uganda
- Indonesia
- Saudi Arabia
- Afghanistan

Interpretive CQ (Being mindful and aware when interacting cross-culturally)
- China
- Chile
- India
- Ireland
- Japan
- Uganda
- Indonesia
- Saudi Arabia
- Afghanistan

Perseverance CQ (Level of interest, drive, and motivation to adapt cross-culturally)
- China
- Chile
- India
- Ireland

- Japan
- Uganda
- Indonesia
- Saudi Arabia
- Afghanistan

Behavioral CQ (Change your verbal and non-verbal actions when you interact cross-culturally)
- China
- Chile
- India
- Ireland
- Japan
- Uganda
- Indonesia
- Saudi Arabia
- Afghanistan

4. LEARNING BY OBSERVING: Go to the mall with someone from another culture. See what he/she is are interested in. Have a dialogue. Comment on behaviors that you see. For example, two people of the same sex holding hands have a certain connotation in the United States, but could mean something else in other cultures.

5. SOLICIT INSIGHT: Share an event that you did not understand that has occurred with someone from another culture. Share it with someone very different from you and with someone from the same culture as the person you observed. Ask for their insights as to why the person acted as they did.

6. PRACTICE SELF-AWARENESS: Become more self-aware; spend time observing your interactions with others. When meeting people, what did they **say** that was a disconnect for you? What would have made you more comfortable? What **physical attributes/appearance** hurt your connection with them or helped? What did they **do** that caused you to push away from them or made you more comfortable? List below where you feel these connections/disconnects fit. Were you comfortable/uncomfortable because something was "right" "wrong" or just "different?"

What he or she **said**:

Right:

Wrong:

Different:

His or her **physical attributes/appearance**:

Right:

Wrong:

Different:

What he or she **did**:

Right:

Wrong:

Different:

After thinking this through, are there areas of education or information that might help you become more comfortable with the people you interacted with for this exercise? (e.g., learn more about the Brazilian style of leadership, learn more about the parameters placed on community for someone of Asian descent, learn why head coverings are so important for Muslim women, learn how Western Caucasians view individuality.)

List these below:

I want to learn more about:

1. _____
_____
_____
_____

2. _____
_____
_____
_____

7. PRACTICE EMPATHY: The next time you are in a store, at a sporting event, or in a restaurant, identify others who look different from you in some significant way. Think about what it may be like to live their lives. Use your powers of observation to get clues about what they may value and how they might spend their time. How might they feel about standing in line, watching a winning team, taking time to eat out? What might they be concerned about? What does this empathy develop your ability to be more patient with people?

8. IDENTIFY TRIGGERS: The Center for Creative Leadership classifies a number of triggers that cause identity frustration and relational conflicts including: differential treatment, assimilation (when the dominant group assumes you will act like them), insults or humiliating acts, different values and simple contact (when anxiety and tension in broader society affect what is going on in your situation).[81] Think about your experiences. What triggers have been more common? What have you done when these triggers have emerged? Discuss these with your mentoring partner to gain another perspective them. How can you work across cultural differences to be more effective in light of knowing what has triggered conflict in the past? How do you respond to people who are very different from you who have just triggered you? What are some things you can do to work through the impending conflict so that you can keep working together?

SECTION 5

MENTORING ACROSS GENDER

"HE SAYS/SHE SAYS"

What difference does gender make and what should you do about it, if anything? There has been a great body of research done related to women and men, their leadership skills, their tendencies, and the value they bring to organizations. Mentoring has been shown to have a great impact on helping women gain more equality in the workforce, especially in the types of leadership to which they aspire. So what difference does this difference make?

A few general differences that have been observed:

WOMEN	MEN
Both hemispheres for language	Primarily left
Navigate with landmarks	Directions (north/south)
Variances/textures	Motion
Manage emotions about stress	Change the circumstances
Failure: Ability is inadequate	Effort is inadequate
Success: Easy task/luck	Ability

With up to 50% of the workforce ready to retire, though postponed by recent financial issues, many people are asking, "Where will the new leaders come from?" As discussed earlier, Generation X and the Millennial will stand in, but for senior leadership you may want to look horizontally instead of vertically.

There are women who can fit the bill right now—they are aware of corporate culture, strategy, and purpose, but they may not see their path to senior leadership. Dr. Lily Benavides studied female executives and found that coaching and mentoring increased the belief that women were more effective in their jobs, improved their ability to develop teams, and increased confidence in themselves as effective leaders. The emotional readiness of the executive, the relationship between she and her mentor, the effectiveness of the feedback, and the overall commitment of the mentoring pair helped keep leadership development moving forward. The primary detriments participating female leaders experienced included lack of organizational and managerial support, the mentoring pair not meeting often enough, and lack of competency of the mentor.[82]

> *"I don't mind living in a man's world as long as I can be a woman in it."* —Marilyn Monroe

Christine Silva, a researcher at Catalyst, points out that the number of women in high corporate positions has flat-lined. The minimal growth of female leadership (around .5%) is similar both south of the US border and in Canada. There are a number of reasons for this. Silva's research shows that it is not just having a mentor that counts, but having a mentor/sponsor in a high position is what helps people advance. Up to half of women in upper level management cite lack of influential mentors as a major barrier to advancement.[83]

People seek out those who are like them, and since there are not as many women in the upper leadership positions, it is difficult for an aspiring female leader to find a suitable mentor. The concern over sexual harassment and the appearance of impropriety reduces the number even further.

Since many of the women in top positions had to work so hard to get there, they often are not willing to reach out and make the path easier for women who follow.

Also, family obligations may make it more difficult to attend the informal relationship building times where mentors may be cultivated. They miss out on opportunities to understand the unstated policies and corporate politics.

Even when they do secure a promotion to high level leadership, they find it to be a very lonely place. Often, they don't want to be stereotyped as a woman who cares only about women's issues. They want to fit in.

These are all large, intimidating barriers that women face! But mentoring can help women prepare for leadership and take full advantage of opportunities they might otherwise miss. The encouragement and support of formal and informal mentoring programs can help women persist through frustrations.

Globally, women's responsibilities continue to affect their ability to step into and stay in leadership positions. Hewlett and Rashid talk about the woman in China who had to leave her job to care for ailing parents, the Arab woman who could not attend a training in the United States because she could not board a plane or stay in a hotel alone, the Brazilian woman who was let go when she announced plans for another child—all going unchecked in the global marketplace.[84]

On the other hand, twenty-six million college-educated multi-nationals entered the professional workforce in 2006. Hewlett and Rashid found that talented women in emerging markets are ahead of the curve in unexpected ways. Studying women in Brazil, Russia, India, China, the United States, and UAE, they found that women in these countries are educated, committed, and ambitious. The primary problems they face come with the responsibilities and restrictions they have as women. The researchers suggest finding talent early and helping them build support networks to fight isolation and gain visibility while achieving business goals.[85]

Mentoring can correct gender bias in the global marketplace by providing advocacy, companionship, role models, support for families in host countries, ties outside the company to clients and communities, and sponsors to help them move through current organizational hierarchies.

GENDER-SPECIFIC RESEARCH

Mentoring: It is so important for women as well as men to have role models, and certain sectors of business do this better than others (religious organizations, academia, science, and the military continue to lag behind).

Mentoring programs should be comprehensive and encouraging learning cultures, and include both genders. For example, Deloitte and Touche's explicit focus on mentoring women has reduced turnover from 26% to 15%, has increased key leadership positions from 14 to 118, and has increased partners and directors from 97 to 368 since 1993.[86] Proctor and Gamble's "Mentor Up" program paired senior male executives with junior female colleagues. Participants in the program have reported enjoying fresh thinking, insights into cross-gender communication, and reduction in the turnover rate by 25% for female workers.[87]

Numerous studies report the benefits of females being mentored by males. For example, in her study on successful women in the U.S. Government, Linda Tysl discovered that these women were highly satisfied and learned significantly from their male mentors.[88] Ann Thompson Moore, found that the majority of highly successful women in business had male mentors who encouraged the confidence of these women and taught them critical career lessons.[89]

On the flip side, the Mentoring Group has also found anecdotal evidence of successful mentoring of males by females. Many reported that their female mentors were "more committed and willing to share experiences than some of their male mentors."[90]

One quick side note: It is important for women to have mentors, but it is also important for them to have **sponsors**. Sponsors are advocates who help highlight their skills and accomplishments to others and promote their abilities to key leadership in the organization in order to advance their careers. Mentors may have a sponsorship role, but a sponsor does not necessarily have to take on the role of mentor. They may just help in the promotion process for deserving candidates.

Both male and female mentors were found to be effective in developing high potential employees, although men have benefitted from this mentoring more than women, as evidenced by their promotions and compensation. What made the most critical difference in levels of advancement, however, was where the mentor was placed in the organization.[91]

> *People tend to incorrectly use the words 'mentor' and 'sponsor' interchangeably. We've all had mentors who have offered advice, but sponsors are the people inside out company who have helped us get to senior levels. Sponsors are what you really need to succeed."*
> *—Gordon Nixon, President & CEO, RBC*

Leadership characteristics: In one study, women as a group were rated higher than men in most of the skills required for leadership (as rated by both men and women), except envisioning "the ability to recognize new opportunities and trends in the environment and develop a new strategic direction for an enterprise."[92]

Women tend to operate from a "power within" or "power with" perspective than "power over." Men rated higher on decisiveness, women on honesty, intelligence, creativity, being outgoing, and compassion. They scored the same on being hardworking and ambitious. Of all the respondents, 69% thought women and men make equally good leaders.[93]

Women work at a steady pace and are not as bothered by inter-ruption. Women care more than men about what others think of them, so at times they may keep quiet in order to keep the peace. Transformational leadership style (making companies more transparent, accountable, and responsive) used by many women is proving to be more effective in business than the more mascu-line transactional approach.[94] Women do not lack ambition as much as they correlate the characteristics associated with ambi-tion to "egotism, selfishness and self-aggrandizement." [95]

On IQ scores, men and women have the same average. Men tend to score higher on spatial ability tests while women tend to score higher on verbal skill and learning.

EQ or emotional intelligence: Five elements make up our emo-tional intelligence, which determines the potential for learning practical skills. The elements are self-awareness, motivation, self-regulation, empathy, and adeptness in relationships. Emotional intelligence is synergistic with cognitive skills—top performers have both. The more complex the job, the more emotional intel-ligence matters, if only because a deficiency here can hinder the use of whatever technical expertise or intellect a person may have."[96] Women scored higher than men on self-management, social awareness, and relationship management. They scored equally on self-awareness.[97]

Women in leadership: About 90% of North Americans are comfortable with women in top leadership positions.[98] Organizations with a high percentage of female corporate officers experienced a 35% higher ROI, and 34% higher total return to shareholders, than those with low percentages of women as corporate officers.[99]

Men are more skilled at self-promoting in a graceful way and project a more secure demeanor. Women are more hesitant about being decisive. Women in general tend to over-prepare, and take action more slowly. Women tend to work as team players and want to be collaborative and supportive, while men will tend toward staying in their specific work position and doing their assigned job.[100]

Women are needed on board leadership due to increased diversity, strategic influence on leadership and decision making, company image, and role modeling and mentoring.[101] Having women in influential positions has been shown to correlate with advantages against competition and long term success of the organization,[102] and 82% Fortune 500 companies have at least one female director, showing an increased profitability with these female directors.[103] Current business trends have highlighted the growing need for softer leadership skills and approaches to power, engaging employees and keeping cool in a crisis.[104] Women may be well poised to take on this challenge.

Unemployment: In 2010, the unemployment rate for men just outpaced that for women at 10.2% vs. 8.2% respectively. Women are on the "brink of becoming the majority of the workforce—

and they start businesses at twice the rate of their male counterparts." [105]

Education/Work: 2009 was the first year more women earned doctoral degrees than men.[106] *USA Today* reported in 2009 that single women aged 22-30 without children earned 8% more than their male counterparts.[107] This may be because women are more likely to graduate high school and college than men and are 1.5 times more likely to earn college or advanced degrees than men.

The number of women exceeded men in the workforce by the end of 2009 (up from 36% in 1972), and 40% are the main bread winners for their families. At the same time, the number of children born to single mothers has leaped from 12% in 1972 to 39% in 2009. The median age for a woman to marry is up from 21 in 1972 to 26 as women stay in careers longer. [108] Women continue to become a strong force in organizations, with a vested interest in making organizational environments work for them. Regardless of these proportions, however, pressures are spread equally: Both men and women report equal amounts of stress in their lives and jobs.

Reverse discrimination exists too. For instance, government agencies in the United States are giving preferential treatment to female-owned businesses in awarding contracts.

Growing up: Research has shown that male brains and female brains are organized differently, with function more compartmentalized in male brains and more globally distributed in female brains.

Girls hear better than boys and they are also more tuned in to color and texture versus location, direction, or speed, which males focus on. (Interestingly, this is most likely why girls prefer dolls and boys trucks.)

Women are less likely to enjoy risk-taking for its own sake and are less impressed with this behavior in others. Men enjoy taking risks for the sake of taking them and admire this behavior in others. Men tend to overestimate their abilities, while women tend to underestimate them.

Aggressive play tends to build relationship with males and tends to hurt relationship with females. Girls who bully do so out of envy, are more socially-skilled than their male bullies and are usually doing well in school. Boys who bully do so out of disgust for others, are not as socially skilled, and are usually doing poorly in school.[109]

Representation in leadership positions: Women hold less than 8% of Fortune 500 highest titles.[110] Women on average are in only 18% of the top leadership positions, even though they exceed men in earning degrees and constitute half or more of the staff or line workers (military excepted).[111] But, the number of women on boards of U.S. corporations is twice that of other western countries, 86% as opposed to 42% in Canada, 25% in United Kingdom, 34% in Australia.[112]

> *"Fear is about power. Exclusion is about power." —Deborah J. Swiss*

Comfort level of women in leadership: Three-fourths of Americans say they would be comfortable with a woman president and 82% with a woman vice-president. The overall comfort level of Americans with women as leaders changed from 77% in 2002 to 90% in 2007.[113] The 2008 elections supported as evidenced by the rise of key politicians like Hillary Clinton, Sarah Palin, and Michelle Obama.

 **IN ACTION**

MENTORING BY BOTH GENDERS

SHE says:

MENTOR: ELISA

One of the most powerful mentoring relationships I have experienced was with my female boss of five years. She modeled amazing speaking skills that I tried to copy. Finally, I got up the courage to ask her to mentor me more formally on my speaking. She kindly agreed. She would come up to me before I was about to speak and ask, "Am I watching this for fun or for feedback?" If I said feedback, then she would come up to me after my talk and ask, "Feedback now or later?" Depending on how I thought I did, I would either listen then or in a day. She would then give me very specific positive and corrective feedback. It helped that she was a woman because she understood things about me that would have been difficult to explain to a man. Her role modeling was easier for me to follow since she was the same gender.

MENTOR: MARK

A wonderful, challenging mentoring relationship I have had was with the male pastor of my church. He took it upon himself to encourage my leadership in the church, and he even challenged me to go back to school to get my master's degree. Without his belief in me and my respect for him, I never would have tried the leadership things I did or been brave enough to go back to school.

HE says:

MENTOR: JANICE

I always thought that I was oblivious to gender lines—until it came to the new hire who became my boss. She was a female. I kept telling myself that I should be bigger than this and that reporting to a woman was not a hit on my masculinity, but there was this nagging feeling that I had somehow failed. And then the organization I was a part of fell into division over strategy that threatened to ruin and/or split the company. My boss modeled a very unique way of dealing with this, disarming people and helping them to communicate honestly. This led to new solutions that actually mended the rift. I am trying to model my leadership style after hers and have asked if she could help me develop more collaborative and authentic leadership skills.

MENTOR: JOHN

I was not close to my family growing up. The dysfunction was too much for me to handle, but in my heart I knew that I needed some kind of male role model. I needed to know how to behave in certain situations, and most importantly, how to raise a family. When I entered graduate school, one of my professors shared his life regularly with the class. I was drawn in. I wanted the passion he had for life and for his family, but I was not in a place to ask for mentoring from anyone. This man began to talk to me after class and, long story short, we entered into a mentoring relationship. Now I cannot imagine a family gathering without him and his family. I learn every day what it means to be a man of integrity from him. I owe him so much.

SECTION 5
BEST PRACTICES

Listening: Promote active listening. When you take the time to really hear each other, it not only builds understanding but also builds a relationship at the same time. Stronger relationships withstand gender challenges much more effectively.

Mentoring: Cross-gender mentoring relationships are a great place to practice clear communication across gender lines. You can learn from even tense interactions, which, when discussed and infused with respect, also help build respectful, productive relationships. Group mentoring can make the best use of the fewer women in top positions who can mentor.

> *"Mentoring is a tool by which women are given access to opportunities and exposure to traditional and alternative models of success."*
> —Stacey Blake-Beard

Stereotyping: Don't let gender stereotypes become self-fulfilling prophecies. Not everyone fits a strict gender stereotype. Things like personality, corporate culture, and upbringing influence behavior. View each person as someone from whom you can learn. This will keep you focused on being curious rather than boxing someone in.

Empowerment: Promote self-confidence through a true appreciation for what both men and women have to uniquely offer.

Support the empowerment of all instead of traditional power-dependent hierarchies. Understand the power of being part of an accepting group. Help men and women find ways to grow and contribute to the organization.

Affirm the contributions of women. Where is collaboration working well and promoting synergies in innovative organizations? Where has relational power worked to further organizational goals? Highlight where a woman's specific leadership skill set fits into the success of the company.

Affirm the contributions of men as well and the cross-gender work that is contributing to the bottom line. Base leadership development and promotions on capability, not gender, while recognizing that both women and men both bring unique skills and attributes to the table.

Make sure mentoring moves toward organizational goals, not just the enhancement of women. Show visible support for female leadership, developing them in practice and in real job situations, not separately.

If organizations reach a critical mass of women in leadership, then women will be evaluated for their skills, not their gender. About a third seems to be what is needed. Ten percent is noteworthy, 20% still remains the exception, and 30% stops being unusual.

> *"Women leaders who are not at peace with their identities or confident in the choices they have made can doubt themselves to the point that they tear down others in an effort to boost their own worth."* —Nancy Beach

Integration: It will help your women and men if you promote the integration of quality of life and work/family initiatives into the workplace. They will be able to bring all of who they are to all of what is going on at work. They will not have to change roles or silo their lives and efforts, which will aid in their overall productivity.

Appreciate differences: Know your strengths as a woman or a man, and work with them. Stop debating and blaming. Work on solutions together. Create a collaborative environment where teamwork and joint decision-making is respected. Use more of a process decision-making model where differences are appreciated and discussed first, and decisions made second.

YOUR TURN

Corbin/Ann

Corbin has just been promoted to Ann's division. His old manager, Steve, was a no-nonsense task master and quick decision-maker. Ann, on the other hand, seems indecisive and unsure of herself. She always asks for others' opinions before making a decision and seems to waste a lot of time talking to the people on her team instead of getting work done. He was excited about his promotion, but now feels like he will be mired in a non-productive environment and have to endure a lack of respect for his manager. What would you say to him?

_____
_____
_____
_____
_____
_____
_____

Georgia/Lane

Georgia and Lane are both sales representatives for a manufacturing company. Georgia has observed Lane being asked to play golf and go to drinks with the other male sales reps. She has noticed that the female sales reps are not included in those invitations, but don't seem to be doing anything with each other either. The men in this organization get promoted at a higher rate than the women. Georgia feels like the social aspect has something to do with it, but doesn't think it is that simple. What would you encourage her to do at this point?

_____

_____

_____

_____

_____

SUGGESTIONS:

Corbin/Ann:

Affirm his identification with his first manager's leadership style. Explain to Corbin that some of what he is observing is actually a strength rather than a weakness in his new supervisor's leadership. Explain the advantages of collaborative leadership and relationship-building as they apply to productivity and long-term progress. Remind him that his new position will require him to step forward and lead more than he may have in the past and that this new environment will allow for this. Encourage them to talk with one another about goals and ambitions.

Georgia/Lane:

Congratulate Georgia on her perceptiveness because something is different. Help her find ways to add a social aspect to more of her peer interactions, regardless of gender. Have Georgia seek out people who can sponsor and advocate for her so that she has the opportunity for advancement outside of social circles.

KEY POINTS/HIGHLIGHTS

- Men and women are different in specific ways. While these differences are on a continuum and not absolute, they can be appreciated for their unique contributions.

- While the positioning of women in the workplace has improved in the past fifty years, women are still under-represented in upper-level leadership. Since studies show that softer power and leadership skills are important to current business success, supporting women in leadership is a key strategy. Mentoring and sponsorship are critical approaches to advancing female leadership.

- Integration of work and life responsibilities helps both genders.

- Women and men both offer unique and valuable characteristics in leadership. There are many positives associated with integration of leadership of both genders.

SO WHAT

WHY THIS WILL MAKE A DIFFERENCE IN YOUR ORGANIZATION

To take full advantage of the positive impact they can have, gender differences should be appreciated and not glossed over. If there is a clear path to leadership for women, everyone wins. Mentoring and sponsorship have been and will continue to be a key strategy to advance women and capitalize on what makes each gender critical to organizational success. Empowerment across the board for both genders encourages and motivates workforces, helping them to be nimble in the current high-speed pace of business.

TAKING IT FORWARD

Take time to write down any reflections, points to remember, or next steps that you will take forward as a result of what you have considered while reading this chapter.

_____

_____

_____

_____

_____

_____

_____

_____

_____

_____

_____

_____

SECTION 5
EXERCISES

1. CONTINUUMS:

Where do you fall on the following scales?

Collaboration ⟵⟶ Solo decision making

Web thinking ⟵⟶ Linear

Task verses ⟵⟶ Relationship

Why did you place yourself where you did? _____
_____
_____

How could you benefit from someone on the opposite end of the
continuums from you? _____
_____
_____

2. PRACTICE TAKING THE SECOND SEAT: As discussed
before, Americans are often not the best listeners. Challenge
yourself for an entire day to put this rule into practice. Record
your observations. What did you learn that you would not have,
had you not taken the time to listen?

_____
_____
_____

In what way(s) do you think this practice might help you in your cross-gender appreciation and work?

_____

_____

_____

3. COMPARTMENTALIZATION VS. INTEGRATION: Men

compartmentalize work more easily than women. This can increase focus and reduce stress. Women tend to integrate their roles as worker, leader, mother, and wife more fully. This can make it easier to be themselves at all times.

What are the disadvantages of each stance?

Compartmentalize: _____

Focus: _____

What are the advantages?

Compartmentalize: _____

Focus: _____

How can you use the advantages to support someone of the opposite gender? _____

_____

_____

_____

_____

CONCLUSION

Though the specifics of mentoring may change, the need for mentoring remains to ensure the personal satisfaction and motivation of employees and the strengthening of your organization's bottom line. We've seen how strongly research shows the correlation between mentoring and positive organizational outcomes—workers need to have support from all levels of leadership and the resources to do their work well.

Mentoring has proven to be a cost-effective human development tool. It also tells your employees that you care, that they matter, and their individual contributions make a difference. Actively nurturing a mentoring culture, informally and formally, will increase the effectiveness of organizational learning, communication, and leadership development. It will improve employee engagement, creativity, and innovation.

With everyone seen as a source of valid perspective and insight, your employees will work more effectively with people who are different from them. Their differences can actually become synergistic, promoting more creative solutions to organizational challenges, and increasing connections so the best outcomes can be found and implemented. Successful mentoring raises the level of trust among your employees to help build an organization that is risk-supportive, failure-tolerant, and thus open to real innovation. A mentoring culture promotes inclusive empowerment of all of your human assets in a time when these assets are so critical to healthy companies.

"What makes a successful corporation is not a great product or a great leader, but a great culture in which people are empowered in creative goodness, innovative beauty, and un-yielding truth."—Leonard Sweet, *Summoned to Lead*

REFERENCES

Allen, T., Finkelstein, l. & Poteet, M. *Designing Workplace Mentoring Programs: An Evidence Based Approach*. Malden, MA: Wiley-Blackwell, 2009.

Arnett, J. & Tanner, J., Eds. *Emerging Adults in America: Coming of Age in the 21st Century*. Washington D.C. : American Psychological Association Press, 2005.

Bajaj, D. "The Invincibelle and the Trust Prompt." *Mentoring in Engineering and Science-Mentornet,* Vol. 1, May 2010.

Bandura, A. *Self-Efficacy: The Exercise of Control.* New York: Freeman, 1997.

Benavides, L. *"The Impact of Executive Coaching on the Organizational Performance of Female Executives."* Doctoral Study, University of San Francisco, 2008.

Biehl, B. *Mentoring: How to Find a Mentor and How to Become One.* 5th Ed. Mt. Dora, FL: Aylen Publishing, 2007.

Buckingham, M. & Clifton, D. *Now Discover your Strengths*. New York, NY: The Free Press, 2001.

Burgess, Z. & Tharenou, P. "Women Board Directors: Characteristics of the Few." *Journal of Business Ethics* (37): 39-49, (2002).

Burmeister, M. *From Boomers to Bloggers: Success Strategies across Generations*. Fairfax, VA: Synergy Press, 2008.

Cassell, C. "The Business Case for Equal Opportunities: Implications for Women in Management," *Women in Management Review,* (12): 11-17 (1997).

Carter, A. "Why Has Coaching Held Up in Recession as Discretionary Development Activity Has Been Cut?" Institute of Employment Studies, March, 2010.

Catalyst. *The CEO View: Women on Corporate Boards.* New York, NY: Catalyst, 1995.

Coughlin, L., Wingard, E. & Hollihan, K. Eds. *Enlightened Power: How Women Are Transforming the Practice of Leadership.* San Francisco, CA: Jossey-Bass, 2005.

Covey, Stephen. *7 Habits of Highly Effective People.* New York, NY: Fireside Books, 1989.

Cross, R., Thomas, R., & Light, D. "How Top Talent Uses Networks and Where Rising Stars Get Trapped." The Network Roundtable (University of Virginia White Paper), 2006.

Crouch, A. "Visualcy: Literacy Is Not the Only Necessity in a Visual Culture." *Christianity Today Online,* posted 5/31/2005. www. christianitytoday.com.

Davenport, T., Harris, J. & Shapiro, J. "Competing on Talent Analytics." *Harvard Business Review*, October 2010.

Dubois, D. *Handbook of Youth Mentoring.* Thousand Oaks, CA: Sage Publications, 2005.

Elmer, D. *Cross Cultural Connections: Stepping Out and Filling in Around the World.* Downers Grove, IL: IVP Academic, 2002.

Ensher, E. & Murphy, S. *Power Mentoring: How Successful Mentors and Protégés Get the Most Out of Their Relationships.* Hoboken, NJ: John Wiley and Sons, 2005.

Erikson, T. *What's Next, Gen X? Keeping Up, Moving Ahead and Getting the Career You Want.* Cambridge, MA: Harvard Business School Press, January 2010.

Erikson, T. *Plugged In: The Generation Y Guide to Thriving at Work*, Cambridge, MA: Harvard Business School Press, October 2008.

Erikson, T. *Retire Retirement: Career Strategies for the Boomer Generation*, Cambridge, MA: Harvard Business School Press, March 2008.

Espinoza, C., Ukleja, M. & Rusch, C. *Managing the Millennials: Discover the Core Competencies for Managing Today's Workforce*. Hoboken, NJ: John Wiley and Sons, 2010.

Fels, A. "Do Women Lack Ambition?" *Harvard Business Review*, April, 2004.

Frankel, L. *See Jane Lead: 99 Ways for Women to Take Charge at Work*. New York, NY: Warner Business Books, 2007.

Gibbs, N. *"What Women Want: A Time Special Report."* *Time Magazine*. Oct. 14, 2009.

Godin, S. *Tribes: We Need You to Lead Us*. New York, NY: Portfolio, 2008.

Goleman, D. *Working with Emotional Intelligence.* New York, NY: Bantam Books, 1998.

Haneberg, L. *Coaching up and Down the Generations*. East Peoria, IL: ASTD, 2010.

Hannum, K., McFeeters, B. & Booysen, L. Eds. *Leading Across Differences*. Hoboken, NJ: John Wiley and Sons, 2010.

Hewlett, Sylvia, & Rashid, Ripa. "The Battle for Female Talent in Emerging Markets." *Harvard Business Review*, May 2010.

Howe, Neil, & Strauss, William. *Millennials Rising: The Next Great Generation*. New York, NY: Random House, 2000.

Keeter, S., & Taylor, P. *The Millennials.* Pew Research Center, December 11, 2009 www.pewresearch.org.

Kowske, B. "The 'Generations' Debate Degenerates: Finding Facts Among the Myths." White Paper Kenexa Research Institute, 2010. www.kenexaresearchinstitute.com.

Kunreuther, F., Kim, H., & Rodriguez, R. *Working across Generations*. San Francisco, CA: Jossey-Bass, 2009.

Lanier, S. *Foreign to Familiar*. Hagerstown, MA: McDougal Publishing, 2000.

Lencioni, P. *The Five Dysfunctions of a Team*. San Francisco, CA: Jossey-Bass, 2002.

Light, J. "Generation Gap: On Their Bosses, Millennials Happier Than Boomers." *Wall Street Journal*, Nov 15, 2010.

Livermore, David. *Cultural Intelligence: Improving your CQ to Engage our Multicultural World*. Grand Rapids, MI: Baker Academic, 2009.

Martin, J. & Schmidt, C. "How to Keep Your Top Talent." *Harvard Business Review*, May 2010.

Medved, M. "When to Use Social Media for Learning." Learning Circuits—ASTD's source for e-learning, 2010.

Meister, J. & Willyerd, K. "Mentoring Millennials." *Harvard Business Review*, May 2010.

Meister, J., & Willyerd, K. "Five Myths and Realities When Considering Using Social Media Inside the Company." People & Strategy: HRPS. Published on www.selectminds.com, 2010.

Moore, A. "Professional African-American Women: Implications for Adult Continuing Education in Career Development." Dissertation: Northern University, 1995.

Nussbaum, S. *American Cultural Baggage: How to Recognize It and Deal with It*. Maryknoll, NY: Orbis Books, 2005.

Peddy, S. *The Art of Mentoring: Lead, Follow and Get Out of the Way*. Houston, TX: Bullion Books, 2001.

Pettigrew, T. F. "The Measurement and Correlates of Category Width as a Cognitive Variable." *Journal of Personality* (26): 532–44 (1958).

Phillips-Jones, L. *The New Mentors and Protégés: How to Succeed with the New Mentoring Partnerships*. Grass Valley, CA: Linda Phillips-Jones Publishing, 2001.

Phillips-Jones, L. *The Mentor's Guide: How to Be the Kind of Mentor You Once Had-or Wish You'd Had.* Grass Valley, CA: The Mentoring Group, 2003.

Porter, E. "Strength Deployment Inventory." Sales Training International. www.salestrainingintl.com. Available for use in a number of languages.

Rath, T. *Strengths Finder: 2.0.* Washington, D.C.: Gallup Press, 2007.

Ruderman, M., Weber, T., Chrobot-Mason, D., Isaacs, R. & Ernst, C. "Triggers of Social Identity." Center for Creative Leadership, White paper presented at the IAIR conference, 2007.

Sax, L. *Why Gender Matters: What Parents and Teachers Need to Know about the Emerging Science of Sex Differences.* New York, NY: Broadway Books, 2005.

Selzer, E. "Effectiveness of a Seminary's Training and Mentoring." *Journal of Research of Christian Education,* Vol.17 (1), 2008.

Sujansky, J. & Ferri-Reed, J. *Keeping the Millennials.* Hoboken, NJ: John Wiley and Sons, 2009.

Swiss, D. *The Male Mind at Work: A Woman's Guide to Working with Men.* New York, NY: Basic Books, 2000.

Tysl, Linda Crawley. "Cross-Gender Mentoring of Successful Women Managers in the United States Government: Toward a Female Model of Mentoring." Dissertation, Northern Illinois University, 1993.

Thomas, David A. "The Truth About Mentoring Minorities: Race Matters." *Harvard Business Review* 79, No. 4 (April 2001): 98-112.

Wang, J. *Entrepreneur Magazine,* March 2010.

White House Project Report: Benchmarking Women's Leadership. Washington, D.C.: November 2009.

Whitworth, L., Kimsey-House, H., & Sandahl, P. *Co-Active Coaching: New Skills for Coaching People Toward Success in Work and Life*. Palo Alto, CA: Davies-Black Publishing, 1998.

Wraight, D. *The Next Wave: Empowering the Generation that Will Change Our World*. Colorado Springs, CO: NavPress, 2007.

Zachary, L. *Creating a Mentoring Culture: The Organization's Guide*. San Francisco, CA: Jossey-Bass, 2005.

ENDNOTES

1. Friedman, T. *The World Is Flat: A Brief History of the Twenty-First Century*. New York, NY: Farrar Strauss & Giroux, 2005.

2. Medved, M. "When to Use Social Media for Learning." Learning Circuits—ASTD's source for e-learning, 2010.

3. Paskowitz, Mark. "Motivational Momentum: How to Inspire Employees after the Honeymoon." Insights for Leadership, Ken Blanchard Companies. www.kenblanchard.com.

4. Carter, A. "Why Has Coaching Held Up in Recession as Discretionary Development Activity Has Been Cut?" Institute of Employment Studies, March 2010.

5. Carter, A. "Why Has Coaching Held Up in Recession as Discretionary Development Activity Has Been Cut?" Institute of Employment Studies, March 2010.

6. As reported by Carter, A. "Why Has Coaching Held Up in Recession as Discretionary Development Activity Has Been Cut?" Institute of Employment Studies, March 2010.

7. Benavides, L. "The Impact of Executive Coaching on the Organizational Performance of Female Executives." Doctoral Study, University of San Francisco, 2008.

8. "Emerging Workforces Study." Interim, reported by ASTD, Fort Lauderdale chapter. www.slideshare.net/nancyreh/Value-of-Mentoring, 1999.

9. "2009 Employee Job Statistics: Understanding the Factors that Make Work Gratifying. Society for Human Resource Management." June, 2009. www.docstoc.com/docs/7934938/Job-Satisfaction-Tables-June-2009.

10. As reported by ASTD, Fort Lauderdale chapter. www.slideshare.net/nancyreh/Value-of-Mentoring, 1999.

11. Benavides, L. "The Impact of Executive Coaching on the Organizational Performance of Female Executives." Doctoral Study, University of San Francisco, 2008.

12. Sherman, A. & Green, J. "Faith-Based Entrepreneurs: A Survey of Earned-Income Ventures by Social Service FBOs in Twelve Cities." www.docstoc.com/docs/9937333/FAITH-BASED-ENTREPRENEURS.

13. Martin, J. & Schmidt, C. *How to Keep Your Top Talent.* Harvard Business Review, May 2010.

14. Carter, A. "Why Has Coaching Held Up in Recession as Discretionary Development Activity Has Been Cut?" Institute of Employment Studies, March 2010.

15. Selzer, E. "Effectiveness of a Seminary's Training and Mentoring." *Journal of Research of Christian Education,* Vol.17 (1), 2008.

16. Zachary, Lois. *Creating a Mentoring Culture: The Organization's Guide.* San Francisco, CA: Jossey-Bass, 2005.

17. Darling, John. "Formalizing Informal Learning." *Q2 Learning* (2009): 2. Web. 15 Feb 2011. <http://www.q2learning.com/collateral/WP-Formalizing_Informal_Learning-20100126.pdf>.

18. Eric Thompson, Founder of Thompson Leadership Development Inc. www.thompsonleadership.com.

19.   Adapted from the more extensive model created by Dr. Linda Phillips-Jones of The Mentoring Group.

20.   http://maypalo.com/2010/10/19/how-to-build-good-relations-at-work

21.   Covey, Stephen. *7 Habits of Highly Effective People*. New York, NY: Fireside Books, 1989.

22.   Espinoza, C., Ukleja, M. & Rusch, C. *Managing the Millennials: Discover the Core Competencies for Managing Today's Workforce*. Hoboken, NJ: John Wiley and Sons, 2010.

23.   Buckingham, M. & Clifton, D. *Now Discover Your Strengths*. New York, NY: The Free Press, 2001.

24.   Buckingham, M. & Clifton, D. *Now Discover Your Strengths*. New York, NY: The Free Press, 2001.

25.   Sujansky, J. "Are Your Best Employees Planning to Jump Ship in 2006?" *KEYGroup Newsletter EZINE*, January 23, 2006. www.keygroupconsulting.com/ezine1-23-06.php.

26.   Meister, J. & Willyerd, K. "Mentoring Millennials." Harvard Business Review, May 2010.

27.   Bandura, A. *Self-Efficacy: The Exercise of Control*. New York: Freeman, 1997.

28.   Dubois, D. *Handbook of Youth Mentoring*. Thousand Oaks, CA: Sage Publications, 2005.

29.   Business Challenges 2008 survey. Noble advisors. Retrieved 4/2/2010. www.noblebusinesssolutions.com/surveyresults.html.

30.   Sujansky, J. & Ferri-Reed, J. *Keeping the Millennials*. Hoboken, NJ: John Wiley and Sons, 2009.

31.   Davenport, T., Harris, J. & Shapiro, J. "Competing on Talent Analytics." *Harvard Business Review*, October 2010.

32. Davenport, T., Harris, J. & Shapiro, J. "Competing on Talent Analytics." *Harvard Business Review,* October 2010.

33. Ortberg, J. "The Gap: The Fractured World of Multi-Generational Church Leadership." *Leadership,* Summer, 2009.

34. Arnett, J. & Tanner, J., Eds. *Emerging Adults in America: Coming of Age in the 21st Century.* Washington D.C. : American Psychological Association Press, 2005.

35. Kowske, B. "The 'Generations' Debate Degenerates: Finding Facts Among the Myths." White Paper Kenexa Research Institute, 2010. www.kenexaresearchinstitute.com.

36. Howe, Neil, & Strauss, William. *Millennials Rising: The Next Great Generation.* New York, NY: Random House, 2000.

37. Burmeister, M. *From Boomers to Bloggers: Success Strategies across Generations.* Fairfax, VA: Synergy Press, 2008.

38. Kinnaman, D. Barna Group. "The Next Generation." Talk Given at MOPS international, 2010. www.barna.org.

39. Burmeister, M. *From Boomers to Bloggers: Success Strategies across Generations.* Fairfax, VA: Synergy Press, 2008.

40. Meister, J. & Willyerd, K. "Mentoring Millennials." *Harvard Business Review,* May 2010.

41. Kinnaman, D. Barna Group. "The Next Generation." Talk Given at MOPS international, 2010. www.barna.org.

42. Crouch, A. *Visualcy: Literacy Is Not the Only Necessity in a Visual Culture. Christianity Today Online.* Posted 5/31/2005. www.christianitytoday.com.

43. Davenport, T., Harris, J. & Shapiro, J. "Competing on Talent Analytics." *Harvard Business Review,* October 2010.

44. Kunreuther, F., Kim, H., & Rodriguez, R. *Working across Generations.* San Francisco, CA: Jossey-Bass, 2009.

45. Burmeister, M. *From Boomers to Bloggers: Success Strategies across Generations*. Fairfax, VA: Synergy Press, 2008.

46. Erikson, T. *What's Next, Gen X? Keeping Up, Moving Ahead and Getting the Career You Want*. Cambridge, MA: Harvard Business School Press, January 2010.

47. Agno, J. *Generation Gap: Gen Y and Boomers. The Wall Street Journal,* September 1, 2010.

48. www.drkathykoch.com.

49. Emelo, R. *Enterprise Mentoring: The Business Side of Social Networking*. Triple Creek Enterprise Mentoring Systems. Friday, 04 June 2010. www.3creek.com.

50. Espinoza, C., Ukleja, M. & Rusch, C. *Managing the Millennials: Discover the Core Competencies for Managing Today's Workforce*. Hoboken, NJ: John Wiley and Sons, 2010.

51. www.dol.gov.

52. Meister, J., & Willyerd, K. "Five Myths and Realities When Considering Using Social Media inside the Company." People & Strategy: HRPS (Chicago, IL) 2010. Published on www.selectminds.com.

53. Light, J. "Generation Gap: On Their Bosses, Millennials Happier Than Boomers." *Wall Street Journal,* Nov 15, 2010.

54. Keeter, S., & Taylor, P. *The Millennials.* Pew Research Center, December 11, 2009 www.pewresearch.org.

55. UCLA study, 2005. www.ucla.edu.

56. Key Findings from New Research on Children's Media Use Barbara Jordan Conference Center, Washington, D.C., 3/9/2005. www.kaisernetwork.org.

57. Cross, R., Thomas, R., & Light, D. "How Top Talent Uses Networks and Where Rising Stars Get Trapped." The Network Roundtable (University of Virginia White Paper), 2006.

58. Meister, J. & Willyerd, K. "Mentoring Millennials." *Harvard Business Review,* May 2010.

59. Burmeister, M. *From Boomers to Bloggers: Success Strategies across Generations.* Fairfax, VA: Synergy Press, 2008.

60. Adapted from Burmeister, M. *From Boomers to Bloggers: Success Strategies across Generations.* Fairfax, VA: Synergy Press, 2008.

61. Erikson, T. *What's Next, Gen X? Keeping Up, Moving Ahead and Getting the Career You Want.* Cambridge, MA: Harvard Business School Press, January 2010.

62. From a lecture through the Christian Leadership Association, Denver, CO Chapter.

63. Abbott, G.N., Stening, B. W., Atkins, P.W.B. and Grant, A.M. (2006), "Coaching Expatriate Managers for Success: Adding Value Beyond Training and Mentoring." *Asia Pacific Journal of Human Resources,* 44, pp.295.

64. Zachary, L. *Creating a Mentoring Culture: The Organization's Guide.* San Francisco, CA: Jossey-Bass, 2005.

65. Institute for Corporate Productivity, "Global Mobility Practices." June 2010 as reported in *Talent Management Magazine,* October 2010.

66. Institute for Corporate Productivity, "Global Mobility Practices." June 2010 as reported in *Talent Management Magazine,* October 2010.

67. Livermore, David. *Cultural Intelligence: Improving your CQ to Engage our Multicultural World.* Grand Rapids, MI: Baker Academic, 2009.

68. Thomas, David A. "The Truth About Mentoring Minorities: Race Matters." *Harvard Business Review* 79, No. 4 (April 2001): 98-112.

69. Thomas, David A. "The Truth About Mentoring Minorities: Race Matters." *Harvard Business Review* 79, No. 4 (April 2001): 98-112.

70. From Naomi Brown, Ph.D., Psychologist at Counseling and Psychological Services (CAPS), Cowell Student Health Service, Stanford University, 1995.

71. Bajaj, D. "The Invincibelle and the Trust Prompt." *Mentoring in Engineering and Science-Mentornet,* Vol. 1, May 2010.

72. Elmer, D. *Cross Cultural Connections: Stepping Out and Filling in Around the World.* Downers Grove, IL: IVP Academic, 2002.

73. Nussbaum, S. *American Cultural Baggage: How to Recognize It and Deal with It.* Maryknoll, NY: Orbis Books, 2005.

74. Lanier, S. *Foreign to Familiar.* Hagerstown, MA: McDougal Publishing, 2000.

75. These ideas were given me in a discussion of cultural differences with Dr. Les Hirst, a cross-cultural mentoring guru.

76. www.geert-hofstede.com.

77. Elmer, D. *Cross Cultural Connections: Stepping Out and Filling in Around the World.* Downers Grove, IL: IVP Academic, 2002.

78. Pew Research as reported in *Leadership* magazine, Fall 2010.

79. Elmer, D. *Cross Cultural Connections: Stepping Out and Filling in Around the World.* Downers Grove, IL: IVP Academic, 2002.

80. Based on the work of T. F. Pettigrew, "The Measurement and Correlates of Category Width as a Cognitive Variable." *Journal of Personality* (26): 532–44 (1958).

81. Ruderman, M., Weber, T., Chrobot-Mason, D., Isaacs, R. & Ernst, C. "Triggers of Social Identity." Center for Creative Leadership, White paper presented at the IAIR conference, 2007.

82. Benavides, L. "The Impact of Executive Coaching on the Organizational Performance of Female Executives." Doctoral Study, University of San Francisco, 2008.

83. Catalyst. *The CEO View: Women on Corporate Boards.* New York, NY: Catalyst, 1995.

84. Hewlett, Sylvia, & Rashid, Ripa. "The Battle for Female Talent in Emerging Markets." *Harvard Business Review*, May 2010.

85. Hewlett, Sylvia, & Rashid, Ripa. "The Battle for Female Talent in Emerging Markets." *Harvard Business Review*, May 2010.

86. Molina, V. S. "Changing the Face of Consulting: the Women's Initiative at Deloitte." *Regional Review,* Q1, 2005.

87. Blake-Beard, S.D. (2005). "The Inextricable Link Between Mentoring and Leadership." In L. Coughlin and E. Wingard (Eds), *Enlightened Power: How Women Are Transforming the Practice of Leadership.* San Francisco, CA: Jossey-Bass.

88. Tysl, Linda Crawley. "Cross-Gender Mentoring of Successful Women Managers in the United States Government: Toward a Female Model of Mentoring." Dissertation, Northern Illinois University, 1993.

89. Moore, A. "Professional African-American Women: Implications for Adult continuing Education in Career Development." Dissertation: Northern University, 1995.

90. Phillips-Jones, L. "The Mentor's Guide: How to be the Kind of Mentor You Once Had-or Wish You'd Had." Grass Valley, CA: The Mentoring Group, 2003.

91. "Mentoring: Necessary but Insufficient for Advancement." Catalyst study, 2010. www.catalyst.org.

92. Ibarra, Herminia, and Otilia Obodaru. "Women and the Vision Thing." *Harvard Business Review* Jan 2009: n. pag. Web. 13 Feb 2011. <http://hbr.org/2009/01/women-and-the-vision-thing/ar/1#>.

93. "White House Project Report: Benchmarking Women's Leadership." Washington, D.C.: November 2009.

94. "White House Project Report: Benchmarking Women's Leadership." Washington, D.C.: November 2009.

95. Fels, A. "Do Women Lack Ambition?" *Harvard Business Review,* April, 2004.

96. Goleman, D. *Working with Emotional Intelligence.* New York, NY: Bantam Books, 1998.

97. Frankel, L. *See Jane Lead: 99 Ways for Women to Take Charge at Work.* New York, NY: Warner Business Books, 2007.

98. Gibbs, N. "What Women Want Now: A Time Special Report." *Time Magazine,* October 14, 2009.

99. "White House Project Report: Benchmarking Women's Leadership." Washington, D.C.: November 2009.

100. Swiss, D. *The Male Mind at Work: A Woman's Guide to Working with Men.* New York, NY: Basic Books, 2000.

101. Burgess, Z. & Tharenou, P. "Women Board Directors: Characteristics of the Few." *Journal of Business Ethics* (37): 39-49, (2002).

102. Cassell, C. "The Business Case for Equal Opportunities: Implications for Women in Management." *Women in Management Review,* (12): 11-17 (1997).

103. Catalyst. *The CEO View: Women on Corporate Boards.* New York, NY: Catalyst, 1995.

104. Nayer, V. "Women and Soft Power in Business." *Harvard Business Review* online, retrieved January 22, 2011 from http://blogs.hbr.org.

105. Wang, J. "Girl Power: Why Women in Business have Suffered fewer Casualties than Men." *Entrepreneur Magazine,* March 2010.

106. www.cgsnet.org.

107. Wiseman, Paul. "Young, Single, Childless Women Out-Earn Male Counterparts." *USA Today* 2 Sep 2009: n. pag. Web. 13 Feb 2011. <http://www.usatoday.com/money/workplace/2010-09-01-single-women_N.htm>.

108. Gibbs, N. "What Women Want: A Time Special Report." *Time Magazine.* Oct. 14, 2009.

109. Sax, L. *Why Gender Matters: What Parents and Teachers Need to Know about the Emerging Science of Sex Differences.* New York, NY: Broadway Books, 2005.

110. Coughlin, L., Wingard, E. & Hollihan, K. Eds. *Enlightened Power: How Women are Transforming the Practice of Leadership.* San Francisco, CA: Jossey-Bass, 2005.

111. *White House Project Report: Benchmarking Women's Leadership.* Washington, D.C.: November 2009.

112. Burgess, Z. & Tharenou, P. "Women Board Directors: Characteristics of the Few." *Journal of Business Ethics* (37): 39-49, (2002).

113. "White House Project Report: Benchmarking Women's Leadership." Washington, D.C.: November 2009.